M000028748

LEADERSHIP
Building Blocks

An insider's guide to success

Dawn McCoy

Flourish
PUBLISHING
GROUP

Midlothian, Virginia

Published by:
Flourish Publishing Group
P.O. Box 5506
Midlothian, Virginia 23112
(877) 210-4049
admin@flourishpublishing.com
www.flourishpublishing.com

ISBN 978-0-9819944-9-9 (pbk.)

Layout and Design: Chandra Guglik

Printed and Bound by Flourish Publishing Group
Printed in the United States of America

Publisher's Cataloging-in-Publication Data

McCoy, Dawn, 1969-
   Leadership Building Blocks: An Insider's Guide to Success/Dawn McCoy.
First edition.
      p. cm.
   LCCN: 2009928353
   ISBN 978-0-9819944-9-9 (pbk.)
   Bibliography: p.
   1. Leadership. 2. Business Management 3. Politics 4. Self-Improvement
I. Title II. Title: An Insider's Guide. III. Title: An Insider's Guide.

For my grandmothers, Alma and Eula Clotelle
For my great-grandmothers, Ethel, Florence, Georgiana, and Lizzie

Because they paved the way

CONTENTS

PART 1 | A VISION

PART 2 | BALANCING ACT

PART 3 | COURAGEOUS FOCUS

PART 4 | DYNAMIC CREATIVITY

PART 5 | EVERYTHING IS GLOBAL

PART 6 | FORTITUDE

PART 7 | GO FOR INFINITE POSSIBILITIES

Foreword

If you're like me you've read your share of books on leadership. All too often though, after I've finished reading, I am left feeling like I've eaten a meal yet don't feel full or satisfied.

Finally, in Dawn McCoy's book, *Leadership Building Blocks,* we have a leadership book that breaks down the behemoth topic of leadership into tasty "bite-sized" pieces that can be clearly understood, easily digested, and most importantly applied immediately. After you finish reading it you will dab the corners of your mouth with a napkin and close it feeling full and very satisfied.

In *Leadership Building Blocks* Dawn has thoroughly analyzed leadership, from top to bottom and inside out. Every concept she presents is grounded in an example, application or story. From her real life public service experience, she illustrates, clarifies, and makes each concept plain and understandable.

Refreshingly straightforward and direct, but still able to touch the heart, Dawn has written a leader's handbook that should be required reading for all leaders. It could duly be nicknamed "every leader's essential guide to effective and high-impact leadership." As a best-selling author, international speaker, organizational development consultant, performance coach, trainer and leadership development expert, it stands as one of the best books I've read on leadership.

Dawn restores hope and honor to leadership, especially in political office. Again and again, throughout *Leadership Building Blocks*, she demonstrates leadership as it should be and leadership as it can be through her living embodiment of the very concepts she champions in her book. As Dawn shares, leadership should be based on giving back. Yes, this is leadership as it should be, and Dawn has given us the map to get there.

Leadership Building Blocks leaves no stone unturned. Whether it's discussing the importance of self-care, having a system for organizing ideas, assessing the dynamics and nuances of forming alliances, handling crises, or what Dawn calls dynamic creativity, *Leadership Building Blocks* covers it.

Apply these powerful building blocks to your leadership experience and I promise you that you will build a solid platform for maximizing your impact, growing your integrity and leadership excellence, and building a lasting leadership legacy.

Debrena Jackson Gandy

Best-selling author of *Sacred Pampering Principles* and *All the Joy You Can Stand*

Speaker, consultant, trainer and leadership development expert

Acknowledgments

My sincere thanks to:

Chandra Guglik, my graphic designer and confidante, for doing what you do so well. You are a marketing spin-doctor and creative genius. www.guglikdesign.com

Tama Kieves, my life and writing coach. Thank you for helping me see the wings I've always had to soar to the highest level of my potential. www.awakeningartistry.com

Jan B. King, my coach and advocate. Your support and insight has been amazing—hoisting me to help bring the final stages of this endeavor to fruition. I'm so grateful! www.eWomenPublishingNetwork.com

William Patterson, my business coach and advisor. Thank you for taking time to provide suggestions, structure, and macro-perspectives with my writing and talent. I'm on my way to becoming a baroness. www.baronseries.com

Debrena Jackson Gandy, my advisor and friend. Thank you for looking out for me and for your countless suggestions and review along the way. www.debrenasworld.com

Tyora Moody, my web designer and social marketing guru. Thank you for your diligence, attention to detail, and flexibility. You have a tremendous talent to share with the world. www.tywebbincreations.com

Shannon Scott, photographer extraordinaire. My fellow lioness: your skills never cease to amaze me! www.shutterflygirl.com

Michelle Chester, my supportive and resourceful editor from EBM Professional Services. You and your team have been dynamic, thorough, and supportive every step of the way. www.ebm-services.com

The Sacramento community: Thank you for the opportunity to serve you and Sacramento city schools. May this book help bring new generations of leadership.

My family and friends: Gramom, Mom, Dad, Katherine, Joe, Dave, Shana, Debra, Jonathan, Audrey, Gloria, and Stephanie, Bryant, and circle of sisters: Lisa, Valerie, Alice, Anita, Wendy, Laura, and Paulette: Thank you for your candor and relentless critique of the manuscript to final product!

Preface

On the eve of the 50th commemorative anniversary of the landmark 1954 Brown vs. Board of Education decision, parents filed a lawsuit against the Sacramento School Board. In January of 2003, just a few weeks into my term as a school trustee, I cast dissenting votes against closure of a historic high school. Who knew that my vote would align me more with the parents than with my school board colleagues?

On the most significant vote of my tenure, I voiced concerns about alleged impropriety with school management and school administrator conflict of interest issues. I asked tough questions and, in turn, became a trailblazer demanding greater accountability with the policymaking process. I just wanted more effective leadership.

After a grand jury investigated and ruled on the closure of Sacramento High School, it was re-opened as a charter school that sparked a continuous debate between the school district and parents as well as business and labor organizations. Nonetheless, I maintained a steadfast commitment to improve policy governance. While public debates and school board meetings between 2002 and 2006 tore apart the community, I stayed focused despite the challenges and chaos created by being inquisitive. I stayed focused because I had gone against the status quo.

During my tenure, I had a clear purpose and achieved many goals. Gracefully, I handled unexpected situations that shaped my legacy. A personal challenge I made to myself since leaving elective office was to share what I learned and how I survived. What I needed others to know was that leadership—the position or office of a leader—is about more than the role itself. On the contrary, it's about giving back and leaving a legacy.

While serving on the school board, there were many out-of-control policy decisions, governance run amuck, and a glaring lack of accountability. These decisions included inadequate protocols that resulted in decision-making without rules and subsequent costly financial implications for the school district. Also, conflicts of interest emerged and the public witnessed lack of personal integrity and systemic accountability regarding management of public funds.

At school board and association trainings, most provided a solid foundation about processes and collaboration. However, what I sought was more than legal mandates, policy analysis framework, and parliamentary procedure. Quite simply: I wanted the gritty truth to be told!

Resources for effective leadership exist but most did not provide a road map about local elected or community leadership positions. Reference guides about political leadership fell short without delivering finesse and refinement. They did not seem to address comprehensive details about hardcore strategies and tactical considerations such as networking and negotiating skills.

Instead, I found books and biographies from noted political spin doctors and former politicians. These resources included authors pontificating about their accomplishments and the policy issues of the day. Accounts from educators and researchers were analytical and presumptuous rather than introspective. Corporate manager guides and executive training offered valuable insight but were not entirely applicable to the public sector.

New to public service and propelled into center stage, my post-candidate experiences and on-the-job training as a freshman board member became my supplemental leadership guide. I had no idea that what I learned would evolve into this book. With limited guidance on public service leadership, I felt compelled to write this account to help ensure that future leaders achieve success.

Taking the reins of a high-profile leadership position must be about more than potential power, but rather about helping others. The reward of public service is about the opportunity to leave a legacy of improving circumstances rather than self-aggrandizement and personal gain. My belief was that effective leaders could do more during and after their tenure by giving back rather than just receiving praise.

Effective leadership skills are essential now more than ever. Leaders often assume their positions without a playbook. The unfortunate result is that leadership is sometimes implemented in a vacuum without clear purpose. No longer can leaders rely on simply being the most powerful, popular, or clever.

To assume a high-profile position is not just about the role itself. On the contrary, leaders must have a vision and global perspective. Leaders must be innovative, accountable, and courageous. At the same time, leaders must exude resilience and humility. Leaders must stay true to their core purpose in order to leave a meaningful legacy. Just imagine: what if every leader knew how to genuinely lead others with definitive goals and vision?

After life as a public servant bringing about systemic change and connecting with people, I wanted to help others learn this too. My role had little value if I did not glean "how to" strategies learned during my experience that I could pass along to rising and current leaders. My goal was to help others understand how to achieve effective leadership. I felt compelled to tell my story in this book, *Leadership Building Blocks: An Insider's Guide to Success*, and to develop the Leadership Building Blocks™ concept that encompasses effective leadership strategies. Leadership Building Blocks are fundamentals that produce action or results that distinguish a leader directing a group toward a specific circumstance or common goal. It is how leaders distinguish themselves through seven building blocks or collective strategies: vision, balance, courage, creativity, global perspectives, fortitude, and infinite possibilities. In this book, I share a handful of leadership experiences and some lifelong reflections within a framework.

Up for re-election in 2006, three possibilities emerged: stay in career politics, reinvent myself as a community activist, or pursue an alternative. I chose the alternative and stepped away from a life as a politician. I made a decision not to run again based on personal family issues and full-time growth opportunities.

Stepping away from this community leadership role, I felt compelled to move beyond that elected position into something else that seemed to have an even greater purpose. Rather than talk about benchmarks for public servant integrity and political system accountability, I wanted to help create them. Instead of basking in the luxury of lifetime benefits that accompany the "honorable" title, I remained humble to reform the image of public servant.

What I came up with for writing this book was unconventional but creative. I draw from my experience in politics dealing with jargon and rhetoric, empty promises, and disingenuous improvements. From these experiences are useful and relevant themes and informal processes that emerged.

In short, my aim is to enlighten, empower, and enrich the lives of others. Included are my insights about how to handle these challenges. Since there had to be a different way than acquiescing to the status quo, what I share highlights essentials for how to become effective in any leadership role. My hope is that this book will go beyond politics or industry to serve as a timeless leadership resource.

Dawn McCoy

How to Use This Book

This book will demystify how you can succeed in any leadership role. With behind-the-scenes examples and practical tools, my goal is to encourage you to apply thorough principles to your leadership path, be it in politics or elsewhere. In this how-to guide, I will inspire you to understand more, get prepared faster, and be more efficient. You will be repeatedly challenged to realize your leadership potential and stay the course.

This book aims to inspire anyone new to leadership, those seeking a leadership post, those already in current roles, or on a lifelong leadership career path. How will you cope when thrust into sudden leadership limelight? How will you gain knowledge to overcome anticipated challenges? What quick training can get you prepared?

Leadership Building Blocks will be a resource for various groups:

• **New Leaders**—The message in this book is especially for first-time and young leaders including high school and college students. Aspiring leaders need guidance to maintain balance, integrity, and focus on the path ahead. In turn, researchers and professors examining public service leadership will benefit from sharing and teaching from insights provided.

• **Current Leaders**—This book is also useful for current leaders—political and non-profit organization management—to help demystify the leadership journey and refine leadership skills. It's also for seasoned leaders well along in their careers. Furthermore, this book will be a useful tool for political campaign workers, political training centers, advocacy and community- and faith-based organizations.

• **Public Servants**—Those seeking opportunities to serve as stewards of the public trust need support to cope with the adjustment to public life. Whether you're a current policymaker, public administrator, or someone thinking about running for public office, *Leadership Building Blocks* is a must-read that will give you the lay of the land.

• **Executives**—Corporate executives and board members require unique support in their respective leadership roles. *Leadership Building Blocks* offers valuable insight to help leaders distinguish themselves to achieve a specific circumstance or common goal. The antidote is a roadmap, per se, to chart a successful journey, outline survival skills, and define how to maintain relationship and accountability. This book will answer your questions and provide the inside scoop.

Leadership Building Blocks is divided into seven sections:

• **Part 1, "A Vision,"** explores how leaders must maintain a vision to transform themselves from ordinary people to extraordinary leaders. This part highlights my leadership journey, outlines Leadership Building Blocks and details the first steps required for any leadership role.

• **Part 2, "Balancing Act,"** outlines key strategies to help you stay balanced during your tenure, including a commitment to self-care and maintaining a supportive network. In this part, we will also review how to effectively manage competing priorities.

• **Part 3, "Courageous Focus,"** delves into the tenacity required when assuming a leadership post. Skills highlighted here are important from the onset whether setting goals or implementing strategic objectives. During your tenure, you must challenge yourself to make bold decisions and go the distance.

• **Part 4, "Dynamic Creativity,"** highlights how you can bring a fresh perspective and innovative thinking to your leadership role. What leadership role would be complete without creative ideas? In this part, you will gain a comprehensive understanding about how to develop these thought processes and action-based skills.

• **Part 5, "Everything is Global,"** walks you through how to develop alliances during any leadership experience. This part highlights the significance of cultivating meaningful relationships vital to your success. How will you build coalitions? What is required to properly engage your community?

• **Part 6, "Fortitude,"** addresses how you will muster the endurance required when dealing with the unexpected. To be an effective leader, you must get out of your comfort zone. With the insight highlighted in this section, you learn how to accomplish more despite shifting landscape and unexpected pitfalls.

• **Part 7, "Go for Infinite Possibilities,"** presents steps required when considering current and alternate leadership options. While the possibilities are endless, how do you address next steps? Do you have a repeat performance? Now that you have successfully managed your leadership role, what will you leave behind? What will you pass along to others?

Key concepts and pictorial images are depicted throughout the book to draw your attention to a situation, behavior, or opportunity:

 Sun—One's unique style

 Priceless Jewel—Gain or show appreciation (i.e., thank you notes, telephone calls)

 Caution Sign—Areas of caution and situations of which to beware

 Rain Cloud—Temporary inconvenience

 Blue Ribbon—Achieve exceptional accolades by going beyond the call of duty

You can read the book in order or consult various chapters as a stand-alone reference tool. Each chapter summarizes key points as leadership secrets. As you use this book as a future guide, it is my hope that you will better understand that your leadership path is yours to define. Take it from me: lessons learned here will lead you on a path of sound judgment for years to come in your leadership journey.

Hopefully this will help you gain as much and more success than I found in a most rewarding calling—leadership and service to others. As an architect of the future, my goal is that you learn from my lessons and make a difference in tomorrow's tomorrow.

A VISION

Effective leadership does not just happen. It requires developing and implementing a solid action plan. In turn, this requires having a vision as you move through several steps to transform you from average citizen into a leadership role. In Part One, you will learn how to maintain a vision, the first step of the Leadership Building Blocks. From my political experience described in Chapter 1, the fundamentals for maintaining a solid leadership framework are outlined. With this backdrop, Chapter 2 offers greater details about the seven Leadership Building Blocks that will help you maintain your focus as a leader. This is essential to do while you're on the job and possibly in the public eye. Chapter 3 sheds light about specific ways you can stay focused, whether you're a novice at the start of your leadership role or more seasoned further along in your leadership journey.

CHAPTER 1:

The Journey

*As a public servant, I learned the art of political
leadership, skillfully managing the business of
government, organizational dynamics, and constantly
changing social interactions. It became a leading role.*

My life forever changed when I took a sharp turn at the leadership stop sign and into the political fast lane. My once well-scripted journey as a community leader and non-profit executive shifted when I was elected to public office.

What I perceived as true leadership was nowhere to be found. Without knowing it, the underbelly of politics was exposed. Firsthand, I came to understand that public service roles are not glamorous like television and movies portray. Veteran politicians purport leadership and make political life appear to be a cakewalk. While most people saw political leaders as celebrities, I found chaos and disarray behind the scenes.

THE ROAD TO LEADERSHIP

My path to elected office was not planned. I had never considered stepping directly into a political leadership role. When a school board seat was vacated, the opportunity to take on a public service role became a possibility. I had to pause. This was a different situation altogether from the advocacy work I had been involved in for more than fifteen years. Marginally, I was involved in local politics promoting citywide college fairs and providing testimonials at local governing board meetings. My role was hardly center-stage. With what I believed in and what I stood for—equity and access to public resources—I entered the political ring.

On my first run for local political office in November 2002, I won a seat to serve as an elected school board trustee on the Sacramento City

Unified School District. Sacramento ranked as the eighth largest district in California and the top fifty largest districts nationwide. At thirty-three years old, I became the youngest African-American woman to serve in the school board's history, and I won in a majority white district of 161,000 constituents, including 46,000 students.

With no prior experience running a high-profile political campaign, a small budget, and limited name identification, friends and family were overjoyed at my accomplishment prevailing in a crowded race of nine candidates vying for three seats. The campaign itself was a grassroots effort run on a limited budget, considering that a run for the seat resembled a citywide race. Well-oiled local campaigns could easily raise more than $50,000. I struggled to raise $30,000. (Most people do not imagine that a school board race is this expensive.) It was the equivalent of running for mayor. At least two-thirds of the expenses covered citywide campaign mailings, voter data rosters, and a lean campaign staff.

A Leading Role

During the early days of my life as a public servant, I learned the art of political leadership, skillfully managing the business of government, organizational dynamics, and constantly changing social interactions. It became a leading role. After I won this at-large, citywide elected position, there were high expectations. As a member of the governing board, I was expected to attend meetings and district events, respond to constituents, and vote on resolutions.

First, the leadership role was not just about voting and serving as an at-large delegate. My position involved taking the initiative to build strategic alliances with community leaders, city organizations, and schools on policy issues, addressing systemic challenges where trends impacted schools and students. My board colleagues and I also initiated a rapport with other school districts on issues of mutual interest. Throughout my tenure, I attended site-based and district-wide events in the Sacramento neighborhoods and the surrounding region.

Second, there was an expectation for me to respond directly to staff and constituent inquiries within the city and some parts of Sacramento

County. In other words, I needed to develop a standard approach to being a good leader. At the time, trustees were at-large and served constituents citywide. There were no specific schools or community groups assigned to each trustee. In short, there was an obligation to respond to inquiries. Moreover, school board trustees were part-time school district employees receiving nominal stipends each month. Trustees did not have staff or offices like other city officials such as city council members or county commissioners and had to be creative in developing a system to manage inquires.

Finally, being a leader meant creating balance between my obligations and personal priorities. More specifically, it meant that I needed to have an innovative time management strategy. Being an effective steward meant keeping my obligation to advocate for education programs and honoring my personal and family time. While there were sometimes three-inch thick binders to review before board meetings, I developed creative strategies over time to streamline expectations.

The Challenge

Taking on my leadership role in office was not all rosy. Without long-standing community ties, I was disappointed to learn just after I assumed my elected post that my intentions came under fire. Many were not familiar with my proven track record of promoting access to postsecondary education. A few board colleagues and members of the community who emerged as political rivals alleged I was an outsider with ulterior motives—running for the board as a climb up the political ladder rather than a bona fide interest in education issues. They did not appreciate my passionate commitment to education since a culture of mistrust in the school district had emerged in years prior to my arrival. Previous school board trustees had been characterized as being reckless leaders upsetting the apple cart. Others got elected to the school board only to quickly seek advancement to other higher political positions such as the City Council.

Likewise, board colleagues and staff dismissed my comments, citing my youth and inexperience. Speaking my convictions, I felt ostracized when tenured board colleagues talked over my inquiries, turned off my microphone, and ignored my requests to speak about systemic inequity and lack of accountability. Some board members and the superintendent at that time were surprised when I asked questions and offered explanations. I reiterated the issues and concerns. I proposed solutions or made objections. Most of the time I gave examples for votes cast and positions I took. It did not take long for me to realize that most of my commentary, however, was perceived as contrary to the school board and district culture. It became clear: it was better to keep quiet than to ask questions. Those who had dared to speak out previously were ostracized. I had to slow down and pause. I had to re-group and understand the unspoken rules.

On more than one occasion, I was chided by the superintendent at that time and some board colleagues for pointing out obvious disparities in standardized testing results between white students and students of color. The statistics were there in black and white; I simply restated the facts. I felt students would be better served if our board more closely examined educational and cultural dynamics in our deliberations. It was an opportunity to find creative solutions to close the widening achievement gap and engage discussions between ethnic-based community leaders and advisory groups. Since I was the rookie, my observations about this glaring shortcoming and recommendations for improvement were taken as criticism by several board colleagues. School district staff, board colleagues, and the superintendent at that time also did not appreciate solutions I offered that were taken as criticism of absent strategic plans to cultivate relationships with ethnic communities. I felt our governing board would be more effective serving the public if we understood the various educational and cultural dynamics.

Other times, some community members ignorantly castigated my voting decisions. Based on my vote against a quick-remedy school closure, for instance, some asked if I really wanted to help youth. I was perplexed since my perspective was to refrain from myopic perspectives and single-student impact and rather to ensure equity for students citywide. Constituents sometimes verbally assaulted me at grocery stores and public events calling me names and sometimes hissing. I did not take it personally, but it shaped my outlook about the work I clearly had cut out for me. Others did not agree with my decisions and took exception with me; they made it personal. Was this really what I had signed up for? How was I expected to deal with all these challenges?

Additionally, local media often vilified my opinions and dissenting votes. Several times, the *Sacramento Bee* chided my inquiries citing that I did not understand the rationale for a significant school closure when I challenged the board majority and superintendent's blanket recommendations. In January 2003, I voted against closing a historic Sacramento high school because I had inquiries about insufficient board policies and potential conflicts of interest among board members and the superintendent. Regardless of how mainstream media sometimes portrayed me, I asked about school board accountability. These questions became part of a grand jury investigation and a public debate over the next four years of my tenure about the high school and related pension plan. A September 17, 2003, *Sacramento Bee* article acknowledged my renegade rookie spirit:

> *Bright light: A political star could be emerging from the Sacramento City school board's executive pension controversy. Her name is Dawn McCoy. She is a new board member. She wasn't on the board when it set up the sweet retirement deals for ex-Superintendent…and other brass, but she knows how to ask tough questions. At Monday's board meeting, she dug into a possible conflict of interest involving the pension authority and its consulting business with charter schools. "We need to understand this," she said.*

From the onset of my role, I asked questions about the decision-making process slowing the board majority with a steamroller-approach to policymaking. Rather than rubberstamp proposals, I simply demanded a process to accurately provide evidence of accurate school district policies, rationale for board decisions, and implications of those actions. I also asked for more adequate public input. Was there such harm with asking for a democratic process in an alleged democratic local governing authority? How could schools be opened or closed without community involvement? How could decisions be made without rules to guide the effort? Why were school district budget cuts proposed at the eleventh hour without appropriate justification, resulting in sweeping job and program elimination? To me, it was about maintaining a real democratic process. It was about being an authentic voice of the people.

THE LIGHT AT THE END OF THE TUNNEL

Shortly after leaving the school board, common leadership themes became clear. It took me a few years but soon I realized valuable life lessons I had learned. These developed into *Leadership Building Blocks: An Insider's Guide to Success*. The concept evolved into effective leader fundamentals based on success I had during my school board tenure. With this concept, common themes are coupled with a non-traditional approach to bring about greater leadership effectiveness.

While I witnessed unparalleled dysfunction at the highest levels of leadership, I simultaneously noticed noble deeds firsthand. Many public servants were quite dedicated through their commitment. They gave readily of their time and resources. Yet, some politicians cut corners on the leadership litmus test making backroom deals, unethical decisions, subtle undermining, and glaring oversights. When I saw the latter, I made a decision to not leave a legacy of politics as usual—just offering the same rhetoric and no solutions.

From my experience as an elected official, I found a deeper understanding about true leadership. I discovered unrealized resilience within myself. What resulted was a reinforced commitment to integrity and achieving success despite adversity, the silver lining in effective leadership. For me, this appreciation for leadership resulted during my focus on service. Becoming a good leader was cultivated through formal development, mentoring, and on-the-job training.

LEADERSHIP SECRETS

- From confusion emerges opportunity to find purpose, solutions, and improvement.

- Overcome challenges by using your prior leadership experiences as points of reference.

- Tenacity and multi-tasking are essential leadership skills to sustain you.

- Find inner resolve by developing a standard approach on your leadership journey.

CHAPTER 2:

Laying the Foundation

Determine if you really want to be in a leadership role.
Otherwise, you might want to reconsider your journey.

It all started when I began doing more than was asked of me. Quite simply, it was a commitment and a desire to be an effective leader. There I was ready to listen with greater sensitivity and to serve with more compassion. How could I have known that my quest for more effective leadership would become my testimony?

As I maneuvered through unforeseen obstacles on the school board with only my chutzpah and survival strategies, my community service role was more than an incidental volunteer or part-time job. On the contrary, I made significant contributions beyond duties-as-assigned.

When I was sworn into office, I was excited about the opportunity to lead and bring my talent to improve Sacramento public education. Just after I took my seat on the school board, however, I felt my enthusiasm diminish. I heard recycled ideas and discussions advocating a silo mentality. I was told by school district administrators and board colleagues to adopt the vision of the superintendent at that time and was discouraged from thinking for myself. I felt confined and pressured to maintain the status quo and myopic perspectives. In public meetings and sometimes behind closed doors I was told to go along with the board majority. During deliberation about a significant school closure vote, I defied traditional board leadership styles by going against the grain—asking questions and requesting rationale for decisions and voting against the board majority and superintendent's recommendations. It occurred to me: Wait, I am not restricted to go along with the majority. I can develop my own perspectives!

I acknowledged that I was not restricted by a ceiling or narrow walls. I would not feel trapped and lose sight of the light beyond the proverbial lid of boxed, unimaginative leadership. From that fateful board decision in 2003 about a significant school closure, it was years later when I realized that this non-traditional approach was the impetus to developing Leadership Building Blocks.

Leadership Building Blocks is a collection of strategies and concepts, whether to a specific circumstance or in general, that is the result or action to distinguish oneself as a leader while directing a group toward a common goal. It includes having vision, balance, courage, creativity, global perspectives, fortitude, and infinite possibilities. Let's take a closer look at each of these qualities essential for any leader.

Vision

Effective leaders must have a vision. The first fundamental of Leadership Building Blocks is imperative and includes several considerations. First, this means setting goals and readjusting priorities, as necessary. Likewise, a leader with a vision focuses on emerging trends and broad perspectives to glean current and prospective action. Second, leaders must maintain visionary, big-picture thinking about organizational mission and goals. In this way, leaders stay ahead of the curve and remain current on day-to-day duties. Next, leaders also take risks and must examine all angles of a situation. By doing this, they simultaneously anticipate the unexpected. Leaders must stay informed about ever-changing organizational financial circumstances, demographic shifts, social implications, and potential economic challenges. In short, leaders must maintain a vision to transform themselves from ordinary people into extraordinary leaders.

Balance

Balance is also a key strategy to maintain effective leadership. Scheduling a range of hours allocated for work and personal obligations varies from day-to-day and over time. The most efficient strategy is to develop a customized action plan rather than a one-size-fits-all strategy. Given shifting dynamics during any leadership role, there are several ways to manage competing priorities. A crucial first step is self-care, for instance, that involves setting a distinction between personal and professional objectives. With this commitment to self-care, leaders help lay the foundation for their success. Another important aspect of maintaining balance is learning how to set parameters and juggle individual, family, social, and organizational priorities. Finally, establishing a supportive network of mentors, peers, and advocates will reinforce effective leadership and underscore the Leadership Building Blocks.

COURAGEOUS FOCUS

The next tenet of the Leadership Building Blocks includes a courageous focus with consideration of the first two fundamentals: a clear vision and sustained balance. Tenacity and self-discipline is required when assuming any leadership post because there are learning curves, risk-taking, and difficult decisions all leaders are faced with, oftentimes against popular beliefs. In addition, leaders must have courage to responsibly assume new levels of authority that sometimes includes oversight for financial data, human capital, and social welfare. Leaders must challenge themselves to take bold decisions and go the distance.

DYNAMIC CREATIVITY

Another fundamental part of successful, effective leadership means implementing creative ideas. Leaders must use their innovation when setting up an effective organizational process, such as an office set-up or filing system. It might also describe how you tactfully approach interaction with others and interpersonal relationship skills. How do you ease into a conversation? How do you thoughtfully distinguish yourself while building collaboration or leading group discussions? Furthermore, leaders must consider creative ways to bring about effective time management given a variety of competing Leadership Building Blocks. In turn, developing a consistent time management system will ensure that leaders align time and energy with priorities.

Global Perspectives

Relationship building is an essential part of leadership success. Developing this Leadership Building Blocks concept involves earning trust and getting along with others, both in general and with consideration about those who differ culturally, socially, and economically. Maintaining global perspectives also involves leaders being committed as team players. Being a team player is about developing and reinforcing alliances, advocates, and allegiances. This can be evident in coalition- and consensus-building. Finally, another aspect of relationship-building involves cultivating protégés and serving as a mentor. Effective leaders help others by sharing their lessons learned and leadership insights.

Fortitude

Having the ability to face the unknown with tenacity and clarity is paramount regardless of the situation. Within the Leadership Building Blocks dynamic, you must manage your reaction on a moment's notice. It means that you are ready to respond and act quickly. In Chapter 15, we will drill down into what makes unknown situations so unique and how to approach these inevitable challenges head on. Likewise, this involves facing ambiguous and sometimes crisis situations. You will need to demonstrate the ability to be resourceful, calm, and focused. In addition, you must demonstrate exemplary verbal, written, and non-verbal communication skills all while mastering protocols, managing the media, and maneuvering in the public eye.

Infinite Possibilities

Whatever you do as a leader serves as the foundation for a next step. You might consider a repeat or successive role. You might also consider an alternative or option outside of this scope. Regardless, you will need to determine a process to guide your deliberation and exit or change strategy. In Chapter 19, we will review the options you might consider when relinquishing your leadership post. Finally, setting infinite possibilities in the context of Leadership Building Blocks clarified in Chapter 20 indicates that you are capping any experience with a foundation for the next leader—leaving a legacy.

 Serving others is an honor and privilege because you bring talents and resources to assist them on a macro-level.

Do You Know the Leadership Building Blocks?

Let's take a look at your first order of business: assessing your leadership skills. How do you size up with your current abilities and examine where you want to be?

Rate Your Leadership Skills

Read through each question and rate your leadership skills on the corresponding scale. Tally your score at the end of the assessment. There are no right or wrong answers and no scientific interpretation. On the contrary, this is an exercise to assess your skill set.

Assume that Less Than Average is defined as zero through two (0–2) times per week, Average is defined as anywhere from two through five (2–5) times per week, and Above Average is more than five times per week. Include examples from both your personal and professional contributions.

1. How would you rate the time you devote to focus on long-term issues and the big picture rather than immediate tasks or objectives?

    ☐ Less Than Average   1 point

    ☐ Average   5 points

    ☐ Above Average   10 points

2. How often do you re-adjust your personal and professional priorities to achieve greater balance resulting in better distribution of a self-care routine (i.e., exercise, hobbies, leisure, and other commitments)?

    ☐ Less Than Average   1 point

    ☐ Average   5 points

    ☐ Above Average   10 points

3. How would you rate your willingness to address sensitive issues and/
   or stand alone in opposition to your peers or constituents?
   - ☐ Less Than Average   1 point
   - ☐ Average   5 points
   - ☐ Above Average   10 points

4. How would you rate your creativity and ability to generate ideas?
   - ☐ Less Than Average   1 point
   - ☐ Average   5 points
   - ☐ Above Average   10 points

5. How often do you build new relationships with people or coalitions
   to expand your personal network?
   - ☐ Less Than Average   1 point
   - ☐ Average   5 points
   - ☐ Above Average   10 points

6. How would you rate your ability to handle the unexpected or crisis
   situations?
   - ☐ Less Than Average   1 point
   - ☐ Average   5 points
   - ☐ Above Average   10 points

7. How often do you ponder alternate or non-traditional possibilities as
   solutions?
   - ☐ Less Than Average   1 point
   - ☐ Average   5 points
   - ☐ Above Average   10 points

These are important questions for you to consider before entering a leadership position.

If you scored 50–70 points, then go for it! You are clearly ready, willing, and able to re-up you membership. If you scored 30–49 points, you might slow down and do some more soul searching. If you scored below 30 points, then you should probably keep notes in an adjacent notebook while you read through *Leadership Building Blocks*. This will help you capture important points and tips about how to be most effective while leading others. Also, after reading through *Leadership Building Blocks*, revaluate yourself with this self-assessment. If you are currently a leader, evaluate yourself according to how effective you have been to date or whether or not you should pursue a different leadership position.

LEADERSHIP SECRETS

After taking the assessment, analyze your results to determine if you really want to be in a leadership role. Otherwise, you might want to reconsider your journey. Here are some areas to consider:

- Are you above average setting a vision for yourself?

- Do you need better time management while balancing or juggling multiple priorities? Do you regularly and readily identify support before assuming a role?

- Do you have average or better courage to take a stand for what you believe in?

- What type of creativity do you bring in your approach to obligations?

- Do you demonstrate tenacity in the face of the unknown?

- Do you look at all aspects of issues without regard to personal bias or preconceived notions?

CHAPTER 3:

Look Into the Light

True leadership is where your vision
intersects with organizational goals.

My eyes were filled with tears when I arrived at my first official board meeting. There, I read the unspoken rules and unwritten fine-print on the school district signpost: Welcome to public office. This is a self-guided tour! Where in the world were those who promised, during my campaign, to hold my hand and get me started? Some mentors and colleagues had promised to help, but policy issues on the docket early in my tenure quickly changed all those good intentions. Flying solo, I tapped into lifelong leadership experiences and learned to quickly apply on-the-job training strategies. Because of a contentious school closure decision initiated weeks before I took office, I had about three weeks to learn the board's protocols. I quickly learned the system basics, the players, and the lay of the land.

Similarly, your job as a new leader includes clearly knowing your vision and goals. You must learn the basics about your role and organization. The time commitment, complexity of issues, and potential for influence are exponential. To be prepared is a proactive way to be an effective leader. In Chapter 2, you discovered the fundamentals about getting acclimated in new territory. With strategies from *Leadership Building Blocks* in mind, you should do your homework, get a system in place, learn the culture and personalities, and develop a team of advisors to help you get established. Later in Chapter 10, you will get helpful suggestions to effectively maintain an organized office system that will help ensure your success.

Your Vision, Should You Choose To Accept It

Get clear about the big picture and your vision. First, focus on your vision, action plan, and goals. With this clarity, identify where your vision and objectives intersect with organizational goals. There's no magic formula. Incorporate your core goals into measurable tasks. Think of it as a personal strategic plan that you revise annually, or as necessary. To help achieve your primary objectives you might develop a three-, six-, or nine-month calendar of goals with corresponding tasks and objectives. In Appendix A, I've outlined what my efforts looked like aligned with *Leadership Building Blocks* in a sample chart. Include your goals and specific daily tasks. This way you can share highlights with your audience and colleagues to keep them informed about your progress toward accomplishing your goals. You can also include a working action item "to do" list that you can review weekly and change accordingly.

On the school board, I constantly restated my vision for greater equity, access, and accountability. As a champion for systemic equity, this meant advocating for this priority rather than addressing unsubstantiated staff budget cut recommendations to eliminate resources supporting the teaching and learning environment. Many times I could not ignore the lack of checks and balances that I observed as unethical policy oversight and staff usurping the board's authority through inadequate recommendations. Greater due diligence was required—more details about my vision and action plan to achieve equity—along with significant time and energy. In the end, it was necessary and worthwhile and my efforts brought about significant improvements.

Second, tracking action plan milestones that align with your vision is essential. For any leader, the first step is to monitor organizational dynamics and cultural changes. On the school board, I demonstrated visionary leadership on behalf of students by watching for what was emerging with several policy issues, most notably the high school reform movement. This included far-reaching district-wide financial and social implications of opening new charter schools. The situation that resulted was low attendance, students from outside the school district displacing Sacramento students, and excess costs at the district's expense. The school district was required to provide facilities and resources for these charter schools, which became more costly than expected.

Third, visionaries must focus on clear goals and reduce all distractions that bring ambiguity. Demonstrating vision is part of Leadership Building Blocks that meant I scoped out all possible angles of an issue for any potential future impact. I anticipated the impact—both positive and negative—for any decision. In other words, as a leader you remain proactive rather than reactive. The opening of more than a dozen charter schools in a given year was of significant concern, but also sidetracked my vision of sound policymaking as an advocate for the teaching and learning of Sacramento city students. These school closure and opening decisions meant a lack of due diligence to examine where there were potential school failures district-wide rather than by individual schools. The cherry-picking of specific schools seemed to indicate a lack of accountability regarding a comprehensive examination of adequate district resources and review of policies on charter school openings and public school closings that guided board decisions. Only later did the school board realize that hasty action would result in lawsuits and legal action. And it was the school district's focus to open more schools while cutting reasonable classroom resources and support staff roles. Perpetually, I challenged myself to stay on track with my goals and vision despite a changing organizational landscape.

Sounding It Out

Getting acclimated with a vision is like a child learning to read by sounding out words vaguely familiar then putting letters of the alphabet together. First, learn how to speak the language in the same way. Identify up front your potential challenges and opportunities. It's best to learn the culture and earn respect from staff and colleagues. If not, you will likely fall prey to a potentially fatal faux pas on the public center stage, or you might be typecast as a troublemaker. State your concerns about issues, but be prudent about voicing issues early in your tenure.

Second, always commit to use good judgment by listening to the discussions and asking questions more than providing commentary. As

I mentioned, some board colleagues were shocked about my inquisitive nature during my first few public meetings. Clearly, as a new member of the school board leadership team, I was not supposed to be asking so many questions. Being a dissenting voice with clearly stated rationale is courageous leadership at its finest. Given the school closure issue that was before the board for a vote, I chose to speak up. When I asked for justified rationale about staff recommendations and apparent staff and board member conflicts of interest, I opened a floodgate of inquiries from the public and some colleagues.

 Asking questions is a powerful tool to gather more information and to shed light on policy issues. Whenever you do so, there will be reactions in support and opposition to your inquiry. Be appropriately inquisitive!

As you get established and understand the system, you will need to make mental notes about potential issues you'd like to improve. In my tenure, it was lack of effective community engagement and accountability. Repeatedly, the school district made futile efforts to authentically engage parents and constituents in school decisions. If I stated this up front, it might have diminished my effectiveness even further. My ability to maneuver and get answers in the system was already impaired since I asked questions. I had bucked the system and board protocols for new board members to take any stance. Fortunately, I was politically savvy enough to be effective in my timing and articulation rather than lambaste colleagues. I made mental notes and added an essential goal: More effective community engagement.

Buy a Vowel

Like many people, I have always enjoyed watching game shows. On *Wheel of Fortune*, contestants try to solve word puzzles by spinning a wheel, allowing them to select a consonant or to buy a vowel with game-show winnings. Without selecting a vowels, solving the puzzle can be quite challenging because all of the corresponding letters are not known in advance. Leadership roles are often no different with tenacity and the ability to guess and solve a problem without all of the answers up front. Learning to survive at the top is a lot like solving these word puzzles. You will ascertain and address issues without the benefit of all the facts and probably minimal insight. Your success will depend upon learning hints from colleagues and allies. You will need to tactfully work your way through the political system and read different personalities. Understanding the puzzle of changing leadership dynamics requires you to figuratively invest in some vowels:

A = Alliances or allies

E = Enemies

I = Issue-specific constituents

O = Outstanding supporters (friends, advisors, mentors, alliances, friends, etc.)

U = Unexpected or pre-existing enemies

All of these types of individuals will be part of your ongoing work as a leader. In political campaign terminology, this alliance is better known as the "kitchen cabinet." It is an informal trusted advisory board that includes supporters, new friends, and mentors. Enemies are both pre-existing—those who are definite foes and those who might have previously been friends but are no longer in your corner. We'll discuss these in Chapter 12. Be prepared to address their concerns and have an appropriate rebuttal handy, if needed. Furthermore, you will have a group of new constituent supporters that include members of your campaign and kitchen cabinet advisory committee, allies and, of course, friends.

YOUR PERSONALITY OR MINE?

Expect that your new leadership role will be challenging and that you will need to determine the leadership style and personality of your colleagues and senior administrative staff. How? Why is this important? In short, you'll be more effective in getting your agenda accomplished and approaching colleagues if you have a clear understanding about their perspectives. More specifically, is their style congenial or more like a power-monger? Are they driven by self-serving behavior, financial profit and public gain, civic duty, or higher political office? How can you use their positioning and style to your advantage? With what you learn, what priorities can you set for yourself and how can you re-tool your strategy?

What did I do? How did I know? What worked? For me, there was a significant learning opportunity to work with a board colleague with whom I differed greatly along partisan and philosophical lines. From the beginning, it was clear that we did not see eye to eye. We both had to pause and learn more about the background of each other in order to find a happy medium for our ongoing professional goals. We met over coffee and pie one day to get better acquainted; I believe that coffee break helped us learn each other's personalities.

Dealing with new personalities does not have to be hard work. As you have done while working with other teams, set aside time to meet with your colleagues on a one-to-one basis to understand each other's goals, leadership style, and possible shared interests. This may provide opportunities for collaboration. In short, mutual understanding and open communication often helps foster a good working relationship. First, review voting records and positions taken by colleagues to assess their political positions and ideology. Likewise, you will want to scope out potential for confrontation and differences between philosophies. Next, you will want to assess real or perceived power to determine your strategy and next series of actions to counter-maneuver their actions.

 Assess your comrades and opponents.

ATTENTION LEADERS!

Modern-day executive leadership is more about building relationships than about taking charge. Any officer or board president must preside at meetings and manage board discussions. You will learn that having an elevated leadership or officer-level role is vital to ensure that the governing board functions effectively.

As I entered my third year on the board, I was elected by my peers to serve as the second vice president. I had earned powerful executive committee privileges to set meeting agendas for board discussion and to ensure collective board member participation. In 2003, before our board had established protocols and before I became second vice president, our board discussions were unregulated discussions. We talked over one another. We ignored each other. Some board members had demonstrable objection and disagreement such as sighs and eye-rolling. At the same time, the public was somewhat disgusted from the perpetual bad habits and immaturity evident from expressions about different opinions and outright belligerence for decisions made. How could anything get accomplished? In my new executive board role, it sometimes felt like I was a traffic cop!

Another interesting dynamic is facilitating open discourse and respect for differing opinions. More intriguing to me was when to be diplomatic while managing board interactions. In my role, I reminded board colleagues to abide by our established protocols for interaction and to hear out differing perspectives. My first year on the school board was challenging because the superintendent at that time was insensitive to opinions that challenged his recommendations. He had forgotten the importance of team building. Since he was the organization's chief officer, he also assumed that the school board worked for him rather than the other way around. My lifelong family role as peacemaker emerged. Many decisions required consensus-building and promoting teamwork to get board resolutions and policy issues approved, so I found ways to re-cap all perspectives in my remarks. Acknowledging what I agreed with, I also cited reasons where I disagreed.

Finding common ground between colleagues who come from different backgrounds, ideologies, and perspectives is imperative in any leadership role. Achieving this takes time. Already I have mentioned the importance of knowing the personalities of your colleagues. It will be vital to know more about their background, family dynamics, and political beliefs. On our board alone, we had different perspectives because of variations in our walk of life and social strata. Our team included a self-employed lawyer, an education consultant, a high school teacher, a state legislative aide, a homemaker and doctor's wife, a former National Football League player and community center executive, and me. Later, after a special 2004 election after one member moved on to City Council and another was not re-elected, we were joined by a chamber of commerce executive and a former migrant farm worker. Here I was—a thirty-something divorcee with no children joining the board. When it came to making decisions, it was no wonder we did not always see eye-to-eye. An effort to find common ground makes leadership exciting and provides a metaphorical well-lit path as you maintain your vision.

LEADERSHIP SECRETS

- Clearly identify and state your vision.
- Learn the protocol, cultural norms, and expectations to guide your strategic maneuvers.
- Ascertain the role other leaders play and how to find common ground.
- Empathize with the philosophical and leadership styles of others.

PART 2

BALANCING ACT

Leadership without balance means you might flounder. Staying on track as a leader means having a supporting network and plan for handling your personal and professional goals. In Part Two, we will identify how to maintain balance. How should every leader prepare and equip him- or herself with Leadership Building Blocks? This part provides guidance about effective leadership essentials. In Chapter 4, we will identify how to maintain balance and create the foundation for sustaining an adequate self-care system. In Chapter 5, you will learn more about the importance of maintaining support systems with allies, family, and friends. Finally, Chapter 6 will shed light on the importance of time management for effective leaders and manage competing priorities.

CHAPTER 4:

Tightrope Walking

Balance is imperative for leadership success.

Circus performers effortlessly walk a tightrope far above a net as they teeter between extreme grace and peril. Audiences peer upward and gasp at how these trained artists maintain balance. What a tremendous feat! Similarly, leaders are tightrope walkers when they balance personal care, social supports, and healthy boundaries. A balanced leader demonstrates a commitment to Leadership Building Blocks by staying on task while being unaffected by obstacles. This requires discipline to remain focused on both the big picture expectations and leadership duties and also personal well-being. Staying grounded meant keeping my senses sharp, head clear, and simultaneously being politically astute, tenacious, and accountable to thousands of constituents. As a steward of the public trust, I remained committed to balance between my public and personal lives. According to B.L. Rayner in *Life of Jefferson*, President Thomas Jefferson once said, "When a man assumes a public trust, he should consider himself as public property."

To stay at the top of your game, you'll need to look at how you have maintained balance in your leadership role. Despite enormous expectations as a leader, you have to stay on track despite the absence of special announcements alerting you to take action. In fact, self-examination and self-correction through personal assessment is up to you. How do you maintain equilibrium in a job likely to call upon your expertise 24 hours-a-day and 7 days-a-week? How do focused leaders find reasonable balance?

The Balancing Act

With any job, the first objective is to maintain a degree of balance by drawing a line in the sand between work and personal lives. In short, this is one aspect of self-care. This is even more important for leaders since you will need proper balance to bring meaning to your work and proper rest leading to recuperation. Balance in any leadership involves constantly shifting roles, peer and other relationships, managing the landscape, and dealing with unexpected circumstances along with attention to self-care. There are expectations to attend meetings and other obligations but also awareness to nurture self. Getting started in politics, I noticed some leaders who were short-circuited, burned out, and even disgruntled. It could have been because they did not have an action plan to stay balanced. That's just not effective leadership.

Without proper balance, negativity, stress, burnout, and physical ailments such as fatigue can emerge. If you do not nurture yourself, the oversight could lead to serious physical and psychological conditions. During my tenure, admittedly I became depressed handling a school district crisis, a sporadic board meeting schedule, and my negative or limited portrayal in the media. It seemed there was no end to the negativity and haphazard schedule. Depression, better known as repressed anger, settled in. Realizing that I just was not myself, after a few months, I created a self-care action plan and daily regimen.

Part of my back-to-balance strategy was aimed at reinforcing my resilience. It started out as sacred time working in my garden every day. Then I took time out for artistic activities and fellowshipping with family and friends. Just a few changes periodically helped bring new meaning to my public service role. Likewise, you'll need to carve out time to quiet the shop talk to just appreciate quiet time and sometimes unplanned conversations.

Precarious Planning

An effective leader must have a self-care program. The reality is that you will experience stress and go through sporadic periods of imbalance between your personal and professional commitments. The key, however, is to maintain an equal focus on both. Focus on a personalized system of healthy activities and you will maintain physical, emotional, and psychological well-being; enhance your health; and limit disease or sickness. Greater self-awareness for leaders means that they exemplify qualities valued by the public including clarity, sincerity, and charisma. Why? With an inner resolve to manage external stress and a dedication to stay healthy, leaders are better prepared to serve others and handle challenges. Think about it. Thought patterns are clear. Limiting extraneous factors allow for focus on decision-making. Without balance and self-care, there is no way for most leaders to keep going without some detrimental health impact.

Self-care also means self-motivation to stay healthy. From various life experiences, I knew the importance of creating balance to buffer the impact of stressful life circumstances. Where did I learn this? Part of my inner resolve came from overcoming childhood asthma, witnessing family members succumb to the devastating effects of obesity, heart disease, and diabetes, and helping myself recover from a family of workaholics. More than that, I found strength to maintain adequate self-care when I survived an unwanted divorce. From that experience, I made it a point to create a solid self-care system and an alliance of support to help me achieve my self-care goal. (The aspects of a personal support system are discussed in Chapter 5.) In my role, I had to constantly renew my focus in order to preserve my energy. It was an essential part to achieve balance.

Self-care is essential to your survival as a new community leader. Taking time out to focus on well-being kept my mind sharp. As part of my routine, I had daily quiet time to reflect about my intentions and accomplishments through exercise, journal entries, relaxing in my garden, and enjoying my favorite music.

Physical care includes proper rest, a nutritious diet, and a commitment to overall fitness. Similarly, psychological and emotional wellness includes maintaining healthy boundaries and rituals producing a positive attitude such as self-affirmations. As a leader, taking care of self is more than the basic necessities such as personal maintenance.

 Make a collection of your favorite quotes and pictures to look through when you need to be encouraged.

Self-Care Checklist

☐ Maintain regular exercise and sleep.

☐ Commit to proper nutrition and balanced diet.

☐ Enjoy your favorite hobbies.

☐ Cultivate your support network.

☐ Pamper yourself (for example, spending a day at the spa, working in a garden, enjoying outdoor activities, etc.).

☐ Keep a positive attitude through self-affirmations.

☐ Process your emotions through journaling.

What Time Is It?

You must make time for yourself. Period! Personal time is that spent for self-care, family and friends, and leisure activities. Put personal time into your calendar so that other events rarely encroach on this time you have set for yourself. After a few years with a sporadic school board schedule, I scheduled dance lessons twice a week and worked my schedule around this. You will need to schedule time away from it all to maximize your effectiveness.

Staying in good health involves exercise, solitude, and periodic downtime for personal renewal. With unexpected crises, a haphazard schedule, and surprise meetings that will arise, you must have some stored energy that will keep you going. Stepping away will be essential to renew your focus and energy. You probably know people with a perpetual cough or cold that required solid rest to completely heal.

Also, look at your physical, emotional/mental, and spiritual balance and dedicate time for activities such as a regular exercise regime, social networking and family functions, and participation in a spiritual practice or religious worship. Author David Kundtz sums it up in one of my favorite books, *Stopping*: "Stopping is taking notice of the space between the notes. Stopping is making the space between the notes important. Stopping is transforming the space between the notes into life-giving, waking up and remembering."

Now more than ever, draw your energy from enjoyable activities and hobbies. I have always found hobbies to be a great source of relaxation: gardening, scrap-booking, playing the piano, and craft-making. Additionally, read a good book or plan a vacation. Keep a roster of quick projects on hand, and, in turn, stay balanced. By the same token, I created notebooks for personal and family maintenance, dancing, and enjoyable activities folders. Since I was pressed for time most days, I developed a process of quickly scanning newspapers and periodicals for lectures, concerts, and performances of interest. Then I would review the list every week or so to see if the event would fit my schedule. The system is simple: Save time, scan publications. Save news clips, schedule later.

Another important part of balance is maintaining healthy boundaries with colleagues and friends. Without healthy boundaries you will inadvertently sacrifice personal care, family time, professional work performance, and lifestyle. Let's first look at how you might guard your personal time.

If you have acquaintances or friendships, be mindful about what personal information you share. Not everyone is politically savvy. Is anything in the life of a leader ever private? No!

Be proactive with family and friends and keep them informed. Kindly advise them about subjects that are off-limits or confidential. Point out conversations that you cannot have such as public criticism of colleagues and your leadership decisions. In the same way, you will be asked to attend numerous events so find balance in your schedule as you make time to support community activities that support your priorities.

Give Me Another Ten!

To burn off steam, relax and enjoy yourself through various healthy outlets. Take ten minutes before or after a meeting appointment to gather your thoughts, transition between appointments, and decompress. These activities will help you keep your thoughts in order. Sometimes, light calisthenics and stretching works best when formal exercise is impossible. I cherished ballroom dancing, hiking, and playing tennis. For me, a modest home gym and dance mirrors made sense to have an anytime exercise plan.

It makes good sense to pause and take care of yourself.
Otherwise, you will be of no help to yourself or others.

Next, consider healthy practices to help you rest and renew. Just think of a musician who inspects an instrument before each performance. Consider the mental acuity of super athletes who go into "the zone" before a sports event. My own experience, for example, included monthly day trips to reconfigure my daily balance and personal care. Sometimes this would be a train ride to Fisherman's Wharf in San Francisco, driving through the Sonoma countryside, or hiking along the Monterey Bay coastline of the Pacific Ocean. I had to stop and pause and listen to my inner voice to keep centered on my work to be done. Likewise, you will want to take time for personal retreats to stay fresh and at your best.

Dusting the Cobwebs and Clearing the Rafters

Sometimes you will have a long day of service. What do you do at the end of the day—go to the gym or sleep it off? How do you handle the potential for exhaustion or spurts of incredible energy? How will you find creative outlets and outcomes with leadership angles you've considered?

Frequently I had insomnia. After confiding in trusted board colleagues from neighboring districts I discovered I was not alone. Many of us would get home after a board meeting only to realize that we replayed events in our minds, re-organized meeting handouts, and prepared follow-up memos. My mind often raced about issues discussed at board meetings, and I scanned alternatives to make sure I had considered all possible solutions. I asked myself questions from all angles of an issue: Should there have been additional amendments to a resolution? Should there have been more thorough analysis provided? The possibilities were endless!

After more than a few marathon meetings lasting until two in the morning, insomnia permeated once sacred regular sleep hours. Rejuvenating for my regular eight-hour work day was not quite the same, and I knew something had to give. I was sacrificing sleep, but lying restless at night pondering meeting preparation and issues to address. I had to be more creative and productive. Instead, I translated the pent up energy into great treadmill workouts or let my cares escape perfecting sonata after sonata pounding on the ivory at the piano. Sometimes I rehearsed salsa dance patterns perfecting the right hand and foot position. Then I turned to often dreaded tasks: cleaning closets and the garage. I created home-spun crafts, painted a room here and there, redecorated a favorite corner. Other times, I just paused to meditate.

I also took time to work in my rose garden and to nurture plants, shrubs, and flowers. For me, this meant taking time to fertilize, prune, water, and nurture in order to yield almost year-round blooming and flourishing greenery. Not only was it a hobby, but it was a commitment to be productive, shifting my ongoing frustrations over situations and board meetings over which I had no control.

In addition, since I am an avid reader and bibliophile, I read books cover to cover. Later, I re-organized my home library by section including biographies, novels, career development, foreign language guides, and reference tools. Thanks to those wee hours, I have developed a pattern of maximizing energy and created an organized cabinet of dream vacations, favorite restaurants, and a list of must-read books.

 Explore creative ways to fill your idle time or unexpected gaps in your schedule.

Finally, why not explore creative, healthy outlets, such as home projects, rather than unsavory alternatives? Revise your goals and clean out filing cabinets. Sort projects and supplies you've been putting off. You may want to carve out time, as your schedule permits, to volunteer somewhere in your community or plan a vacation. Suddenly home projects can be lots of fun! Some creative projects include filing and sorting, organizing, cleaning, and revising.

LEADERSHIP SECRETS

- Maintain balance between work and personal obligations to prevent burnout or ailments.

- Develop a self-care program to ensure your survival.

- Commit to self-care strategies that bring balance and focus.

- Carve out daily time to decompress before and after meetings.

- Allocate, where you can, time for social activities and creative outlets.

- Maintain healthy boundaries, and guard your personal time and obligations.

CHAPTER 5:

Where Is Your Safety Net?

"Lots of people want to ride with you in the limo, but what you want is someone who will take the bus with you when the limo breaks down."
—*Anonymous*

Where and who do leaders go to for support? With new extraordinary expectations—public attention, media calls, and constituent complaints—where do leaders turn for advice and comfort? Having a support system means having people important to you—family, friends, mentors, and trusted colleagues—who can be there as advocates when you assume the reins of authority. A solid support system will be essential to your success on the job and to help you achieve balance. Having a viable, healthy support system is important because you will need a safe-haven in order to reinvigorate on a regular basis. Why?

On this journey, you will encounter numerous challenges, disappointments, and judgment, among other unhealthy considerations. You will also need support when you feel overwhelmed, frustrated, unsupported, or misunderstood. You will need a reminder that you are not alone. Depending on your personal style, you will need to check in with your support system on a daily or weekly basis depending on your relationship or availability. How can you build a consistent safety net, a support system?

CATCH ME! I'M FALLING!

As soon as you ponder any leadership role, share details about your anticipated obligations with close family, friends, and advisors. At the heart of your support system will be the obvious people—family members and your significant other or spouse. Their reinforcement and encouragement means having a sounding board, solace, and an advocate before your leadership role. Have a discussion about the impact of that role on your schedules and social interaction. Always remember that your family is your "fan club" and that they are learning along with you about how to best support you in your role. Some of my favorite cousins were great listeners who were on the receiving end of my exasperated post-meeting frustrations. On more than a few occasions, they offered timely words of encouragement. I can remember getting home in the wee hours from a school board meeting completely weary and discouraged. Sleep was not even a consideration, but a few kind words that I was making a difference assuaged my woes and were more valuable than the price of gold.

 Be sure to send along a note of gratitude for those who provide support, a listening ear, or helpful unsolicited advice.

Let your support network know about expectations for your time commitments, community obligations, and possibly greater media and public attention. Explain your duties and offer suggestions about how they can help you. This will help them understand the nature of your job, the magnitude of the role, and also the need you may have to have a safe place away from the center stage. You will both have a clear idea about helpful telephone calls, email messages, and simply friendly notes. You can ask for support that reinforces the positive and avoid criticism or re-hashing of issues. For me, it meant getting clarity by stepping away occasionally from policy analysis and constituent inquiries that demanded my time and energy.

Be sure to celebrate various small victories and personal triumphs with your circle of support. Share with them projects you are working on. For me, sometimes this meant letting family know that I was keeping my nose to the grindstone working on the systemic issues rather than getting caught in the political fray.

 Cherish both small victories and peaceful moments.

Finally, be mindful of each other's commitments. More than likely you and your family have multiple—and sometimes competing—priorities. Periodically discuss each other's expectations and how you anticipate carving out time for family priorities. It will also be easier to weave this support function into your schedules if you approach the task with mindfulness about attending standing events you had prior to your leadership role.

One standing commitment I had was to attend an annual family reunion where I had no title other than cousin, daughter, granddaughter, niece, or descendent of "so-and-so." Who I was in the world had no relevance. Only the elders presiding and the ancestors at a nearby cemetery were the ones with official titles. I always appreciated annual family reunion gatherings coupled with a journey to my grandmother's house. Most people appreciate a visit to their grandmother's house, but the times I scheduled a journey away from Sacramento to her house and for the family gathering were priceless. I found tranquility after indulging in a plate of her famous cheese grits or a delicious turkey wing dinner. But it was more than that. All the complexities about politics, leadership, and public policy issues disappeared with her comfort and words of wisdom about life. What she imparted was not always profound, but it was timely and transcended anything that seemingly mattered on the center stage of the school board.

A Friend in Need Is a Friend Indeed

Another part of your support network will include your circle of friends. Ask those closest to you to make time for fellowship away from peering eyes. This will be extremely helpful during your tenure under the microscope because it allows you to be yourself without leadership circle expectations. For me, cherished time included getting together for a good cry, a belly laugh, and just having a listening ear. Having a peaceful tea party with friends one sunny summer afternoon in my garden meant non-stop laughter and girl talk that was quite refreshing. My only expectations were to refill the cucumber sandwich tray and lemonade pitcher.

The more you get into your work or if the demands on your contribution change, as they did for me, the more you will need a reliable support network. Given the increased expectations, getting support will be more important than ever to help create structure. You will serve yourself well by scheduling lunch or coffee dates, planning road and beach trips, and regular movie nights. A friend and I made it a point to schedule getaways to various music concerts as far in advance as our schedules allowed. Here, we could laugh and carry on about the latest or just sit back and appreciate the artists.

Finally, another part of your circle will include your mentors, advisors, and those among your most trusted colleagues. On any given day, you might need advice or insight about decisions or next steps that you might otherwise determine on your own. As with any role, you are gaining insight from someone who has been in a similar situation, has expertise in a specific area, or has some background handling a matter.

As an elected official, I often sought input from other elected officials and school board trustees who I admired or who preceded me handling similar policy issues or circumstances. Other times I consulted community advocates and professors over standing coffee appointments where they provided perspectives about specific policy or protocol. There is no magic potion to bring answers to questions asked since only you will know the best course of action to take. Sometimes, however, additional perspective or a new understanding may emerge from discussions with an advisor.

Similar to how you will create ongoing dialogue with friends and family, schedule time to meet with your trusted advisors to glean their insight on specific topics. Their assistance will be vital to your ongoing success and even more meaningful if they have prior experiences that will help you overcome some challenge.

It's Business, Not Personal

With consistent demands on your time, carve out time for handling personal matters. It will help you maintain balance. Be sure to spend time with advocates where you talk about anything but your leadership duties. You will need to have time away from official matters to rejuvenate.

It's always easier to safeguard your personal space ahead of time. Scheduling standard coffee dates with friends reinforced my friendships. Avoid canceling these appointments except for extreme reasons. Rearranging your personal commitments might have unintended consequences leading to unnecessary doubt about your sincerity. By the same token, be unapologetic to those who cannot accept your leadership responsibility.

Can We Talk?

Be adamant about parameters with the public and your support network. Sometimes you just want to talk about the issues discussed in public forums. Other times you would rather not. That's okay. But, occasionally your closest colleagues are interested to know more than what the public sees. Gently remind friends that you have taken an oath and are bound by confidentiality agreements to not discuss matters beyond those shared in public. Just don't do it!

Likewise, put a hedge around your personal life. Remind professional colleagues who press you to share more about your personal life. Only share what and when you feel comfortable putting out there for public consumption. For me, my mother's declining health was particularly painful to discuss. I gently reminded inquiring minds that she was doing as best as we could expect and I left it at that. Only you will determine the parameters of comfort sharing information in both your public or private lives.

Loose Lips Indeed Sink Ships

Being a leader who others follow involves building trust. Without it, you cannot garner support and the erosion of this leads to misgivings and sometimes gossip as people attempt to gain some insight and realign trust relationships. So you heard some juicy gossip, right? The bottom line: Never start gossip or rumors and never share gossip and rumors. Acknowledge what you've heard by saying "How interesting" or "I didn't know that," but never engage in this negative, unhealthy behavior. Not only does it bring your spirits down but it also reminds you that whoever is sharing this information with you will share your business and private conversations and business with others.

It is your job on your path to success to rise above the fray. How should you do this? Deflect gossip by changing the subject. Distract yourself or the other person. Simply excuse yourself from the conversation. It's never a good idea to bad mouth your colleagues regarding their character, dissenting votes, or the issues on which you may disagree. I've seen this done and if you have even a slight slip of the tongue it can be disastrous!

LEADERSHIP SECRETS

- Clarify for your supporters how they can listen, encourage you, and be an advocate.

- Identify and maintain a close circle of friends who can be your most trusted allies.

- Earmark time to spend with your network.

- Pause to cherish time spent and honor scheduled commitments.

CHAPTER 6:

Juggling Acts

True leadership success comes from managing
multiple priorities simultaneously.

Multitasking is another important aspect of strategies learned with Leadership Building Blocks in mind. I know because I learned this skill from my parents. With almost a half dozen cross-country road trips by the time I was ten years old, my siblings and I got used to shifting priorities. We moved around the country during the early 1970s. For the most part, moving was in pursuit of a handful of coveted higher education opportunities my father had for medical school and subsequent specialist training. At the same time my mother finished her graduate degree. What followed were annual vacations to visit relatives in other states and quick adjustments to new neighborhoods and local culture. As the eldest child, it did not occurred to me at the time that I was learning to balance multiple tasks. It came naturally. It was also just expected that I did. These early lessons where I adjusted to change set the groundwork for how I evolved as a leader. How do leaders successfully handle shifting priorities?

To learn how to be the most effective leader managing competing goals, you'll need to assess how to handle your goals based on your personality and your prior leadership experiences. For some, your leadership role might encroach into your personal life. Or you may need to overcome an unexpected crisis. This chapter includes some useful insights to guide your journey.

MANAGING PRIORITIES

The movement of objects in rhythmic pattern through the air is the art of juggling, often for entertainment purposes. What comes to mind is a performer throwing and catching objects such as balls or bowling pins simultaneously. A fascinating detail is the number and variety of objects skillfully handled at one time. The more objects manipulated at a time while moving—rather than stationary—is also what makes the art form so complex. Interestingly enough, juggling metaphorically describes the process of refocusing attention between priorities—responsibilities, and expectations—at the same time.

For a leader, this means managing goals and tasks, often numerous competing priorities and ongoing issues. Work must be done. Issues require your interpretation, action, and perspective. Your clients and constituents need answers. Everything is due by tomorrow. Despite your own personal feelings and/or obligations, those you lead will always expect you to be readily available to listen, smile, and jump into action. How do you manage this? Is there a formula for success?

First, organize priorities into various categories, the objects that are juggled. In my role, for instance, I noted personal objectives, policy issues, crises situations, and interpersonal relations. I joined the board during high school reform (policy issue) and a focus on charter school implementation to achieve equity with questionable effective governance (personal objectives), cast with a backdrop of impropriety (crisis situation), my own family medical emergency (crisis situation), and an attempt to reinforce board and community relations (interpersonal relations). While I'm oversimplifying these categories, my intent will help clarify what is often perceived as competing obligations. This is how the "juggle struggle" emerges for so many. Through this, you will better understand the expectations associated that will help you manage priorities.

Second, develop a system to help you stay focused. While I could have been overwhelmed by just one area alone, I developed a matrix to help me stay focused. In the grid, I listed tasks and demands for my time down the side of the page, and across the top of the page I labeled columns with "important," "urgent," and "non-essential" to prioritize my time. Then I inserted checkmarks for each task. After reviewing where the most checkmarks landed, it became clear where I needed to shift my focus. Before I developed this, I felt the constant strain on my time. My energy was always drained running to respond in helter-skelter fashion without an essential reason for actions. Without question, it helped me handle several areas at once and guided my daily tasks. What I found along my journey were various ways to approach each task.

 The sooner you get yourself organized, the faster you will maximize your time and energy.

PRECISION AND PANACHE

Since you are under a microscope, always play nice. You have several obligations as a leader to demonstrate sportsmanship even when others— colleagues, constituents, or the media—are throwing mud at you. First, this means having a poker face or looking deadpan rather than cringing, rolling your eyes, or sighing. Not only is it unprofessional, but it demonstrates lack of maturity and the ability to respect differing opinions. Believe me. I watched others show more than enough unsophisticated gestures and behaviors when they disagreed with someone else. Can you imagine the delight a political cartoonist would have had with our board proceedings? Of course, I wanted to show some emotion on occasion, too.

Second, keep up appearances, since it will be an important part of your role. During the most contentious times of board high school reform discussions and meetings, there was still an expectation to attend community meetings and events. At one point, I had reached a level of maximum capacity. Giving one-hundred-and-ten percent to my day job and public service duties, I realized something had to give. Many constituents and colleagues were curious when I failed to bring my A-game in either venue. Some cast aspersions and judgment. Truth be told, I had bigger concerns on my mind.

GRACE UNDER PRESSURE

Sometimes, the most important thing is recognizing when you cannot keep all the balls in the air. At the beginning of 2004, I took on a new role dealing with serious family health challenges. Close friends knew about my increased responsibility to help manage my mother's declining health. With her debilitating diabetes and other complications, she needed more serious medical treatment. Driving an average of six hours round trip from my house to her house, I had to buckle down and do a juggling act with handling her medical care and my own schedule. I was faced with getting her to doctor appointments and helping with chores.

Then, I had to manage getting back to town for meetings and regular appearances. In all honesty, I was finding it more difficult to do both jobs—public service and full-time work—and create balance to take care of myself. In fact, it was almost impossible. Board meetings were often scheduled on a weekly rather than biweekly basis. My full-time job duties required me to visit financial aid offices at Northern California colleges and universities. In other words, day trips and overnight travel for work became complicated with my community and family obligations.

In March 2006, I wrote a letter to supporters announcing my intent to not run for reelection in November 2006. Part of my decision was based on my need to be more attentive to my mother's health and another part was based on the level of effectiveness I had reached. Only after my letter became public did people come to see me as a real person with personal priorities. I was no longer simply their representative addressing their policy concerns and resolving problems.

When I stopped trying to juggle every priority, expected or unexpected, I paused to put my own health and family health concerns in perspective. At that moment, I realized a higher priority than my career. There was a greater purpose in my own welfare and that of my loved ones, especially my mother with her declining health. Those reasons alone compelled me to drop most of the proverbial balls I was tossing to instead focus on the essential.

Pause to examine all that you are managing in your personal and professional lives. After you assess and re-evaluate your priorities, proceed with taking steps to implement each one at a time.

DEXTERITY

Surviving long meetings and back-to-back appointments is only possible with advance planning and re-prioritizing. For me, I just barely maintained reasonable health running at a break-neck pace and eating on the go. In fact, it was only after almost complete delirium on more than one occasion that I realized something had to change. I distinctly remember: I was under the daze of bright lights and television cameras at yet another marathon board meeting. I kept my game face on but kept wondering if I might step out briefly to order a Domino's pizza. What if I slipped out to have some friends whisk me away for an evening of relaxation and laughter? When my stomach growled back at me, I refocused on the policy discussion at hand. I knew that to become a more effective policymaker, I had to prepare a backup meal plan accordingly. My personal expectation of reasonable leadership meant that lethargy and not paying attention were not options.

I learned the hard way after sitting through six-hour marathon board meetings without food and a good night's rest. To help sustain my energy levels, I toted candies, dried fruit, mints, and sometimes fresh vegetables in case meetings ran longer than expected or if I did not have time for a meal between appointments. Sometimes these treats came in handy to share with others. Doing this, you can maximize your time while you're "on."

 You may want to consider adding basic rations to your office-on-wheels including a supply of office materials and light refreshments.

LEADERSHIP SECRETS

- Get clarity about your priorities and expectations.

- Develop a system to prioritize your tasks and objectives.

- Maintain your focus, remain professional, and keep up appearances.

- Be flexible and prepared according to your personal leadership expectations.

PART 3

COURAGEOUS FOCUS

Part Three highlights strategies that will be essential throughout your tenure. As a leader, you will face a variety of challenges. Chapter 7 addresses the various ways you can demonstrate courage. Chapter 8 addresses repetition and self-discipline required to achieve positive outcomes when the unexpected inevitably happens. How will you cultivate inner focus? How will you review the landscape during your leadership role? In Chapter 9, you will learn more about strategies to help you overcome adversity. We will review what it takes to really go the distance.

CHAPTER 7:
Trailblazing and Blazing Trails

Effective leadership requires audacity to go
where there is no existing pathway.

When my board tenure began and I trekked into uncharted territory, I found unrealized courage without even knowing it. Contentious meetings drew almost one thousand people who expressed opposition or support for school board deliberations regarding the closure of the 100-year-old Sacramento High School. Thrust into the center stage of the political arena as part of the local elected leadership, it was like being a tourist caught in New York City's Grand Central Station at rush hour.

Questions I had of the superintendent and staff drew both criticism and praise. My concerns were about decision-making without current rules to guide board action. Board colleagues were flabbergasted when I dared to take a dissenting position just months into my political career. Simultaneously and quite unintentionally I had both established my unique leadership path and set a new course for board governance.

Along the leadership path, you will encounter the unexpected. There will be opportunities to pave the way toward new understandings, sometimes based upon your prior experiences. Other times you will discover that your style brings forth a new perspective or you discover a different way to accomplish a traditional task. Most leaders are trailblazers who set a new route and also leave behind an imprint or indication of having been there, sometimes through overcoming adversity.

As a leader, you will deal with more than the new position of authority itself but also acknowledge the opportunity to be an example, to be a pioneer. On the school board, for instance, my goals were to find solutions to failing schools, to address systemic district inequity, and to address inadequate resources district-wide. In fact, my role became more about dealing with effective governance than the policy issues. Here are a few ways I became a trailblazer and traits you might ponder as you lead with the fundamentals of Leadership Building Blocks.

UNEXPLORED TERRAIN

Every leader paves new pathways in both deliberate and unintended fashion. Sometimes you will chance upon an innovative pathway; other times you will create history unintentionally through persistence. To explore this unfamiliar territory means taking a chance even if never done before. In my role, I took a stand contrary to the board majority regarding the decision to close a historical high school after it was deemed a failure. School district administrators had concluded that the closure was necessary based on apparently unsuccessful programs and a floundering six-month reform effort. My persistent questions created unprecedented political tension between board members and leadership on my part as a freshman politician: Is there a district policy about closing schools for charter school consideration? What guides board protocols for discussion? What caused the school to be deemed a failure and require conversion to a charter school? How would the district maintain accountability for the students displaced by this decision? Is this decision absolutely necessary and the only possibility? How does the district maintain effective governance and policies? What are the implications? What if parents and the community object to the decision?

 As a leader, you will undoubtedly have new territory to explore. This will require that you step out of the traditional pathway and courageously set your own.

DELIBERATE EFFORTS

As a leader, you must also be deliberate in your quest. For me, I asked repeated questions. Despite my polite requests for more thorough policy analysis, the school closed and converted into a charter school. The mandate led to more than a dozen new district charter schools as part of a national high school reform movement over the next eighteen months. Nonetheless, the school closure decision led to a lawsuit from parents against the board, a divided community, a public campaign to recall board members voting for the school's closure, and an exhaustive grand jury inquiry about conflicts of interest that went on for several years.

I objected to the expeditious proceedings and essentially thwarted the process by seeking a formal review of lacking documentation. I recall the moment I consciously decided to not just go along with the majority. As I took a deep breath, I knew that being proactive and gathering more information before making a decision about the school closure would change everything about how I was perceived. Sadly, my stance also undermined fledgling community relationships and political ties I had established on the campaign trail. Specifically, my observations were regarding school closure implications, the cause of the school's failing status, and lacking systemic due diligence. It seemed the entire process required an overhaul to really address the needs of all students. It became clear: I had to chart new territory by challenging the superintendent and the staff's school closure recommendations.

Just months on the board, I was willing to risk new alliances to publicly ask probing questions seeking clarity before casting my vote. There was no grand formula guiding me in what felt like no man's land. Despite wincing eyes, furrowed brows, and suspicious glances directed at me from nearly every corner, I asked pointed questions. Yes, these reactions were from community members, school district staff, and board colleagues alike. It felt to me that I had done my due diligence. With all this gumption, now what was I supposed to do at the crossroads?

Popcorn Along the Trail

With minimal orientation, marginal support from colleagues, and only my own vocal observations, I hit the ground running. From these early experiences at the helm of public service leadership, I knew a game plan was essential. A popcorn trail to guide my every action would have been ideal. Instead, I had to create a thorough, focused strategy with definitive action steps. It had to address both the systemic education challenges and also policy issues. Rather than a linear plan based on my campaign platform, I quickly amended my goals into a three-pronged approach—a commitment to effective governance, accountability, and a focus on systemic reform. In just three months, I had gone from quietly and slowly adjusting to a high-profile public service leadership role to lobbing loaded fireball questions at board meetings. Not exactly what I had planned! Inside, I further resolved to maintain accountability with my good name on the line. I made a commitment to make the system better before leaving office and not to leave a legacy of politics as usual. So, how will you be ready for any dusty trail? What will help you be prepared for the job on day one?

LEADERSHIP SECRETS

- Be a visionary who is prepared with big-picture and inclusive thinking.

- Determine how you will reinforce personal accountability and integrity.

- Build relationships that are essential to any successful leadership journey.

- Reinforce strategies to master the art form of meaningful influence and advocacy.

CHAPTER 8:

Practice Makes Perfect

*Developing leadership success includes staying the
course from start to finish and developing a routine.*

As a classically trained pianist, I learned during childhood how consistent practice and repetition improves competence. The more I practiced, the more I improved. As I got better, the more advanced musical compositions I played. At the same time, I developed self-discipline that became a valuable lifelong skill and an essential part of various leadership roles. What also became clear to me was that careless practice or none at all made my musical talent decline. The point is simple: The more you exercise your skills, the better you get.

In the same way, you will learn how to become a better leader with practice. With Leadership Building Blocks in mind, it takes guidance, self-motivation, and self-correction. Sometimes you call upon others. On other occasions, you might look at success you had in your prior professional and personal leadership roles. Until you find a comfortable stride that works, you might ask yourself some questions: How do leaders learn how to become better at what they do? Is there some magic potion, or is it innate?

Quite simply, leaders get better at being leaders by striving for a specific goal, staying focused, implementing a routine, and repetition. Here are a few examples of how to improve as a leader.

Stay Focused!

Without question, there are many tasks that require your undivided attention and focus. None was more compelling for me than learning to ride a motorcycle, where it was not the motorcycle and road conditions that contributed to my ability to improve as a rider, but my focus. The instructor shared the basics and details regarding a comfortable traveling speed that required the twist of the throttle and simultaneous release of the clutch. Off I went on the training course with just a few days of practice! Through the series of repetitive and strategic motorcycle moves, I quickly became a comfortable beginner rider and went on to get my motorcycle license. Serving in a leadership role is no different. It requires varying degrees of measured speed, skilled maneuvering, and timing in varied circumstances. Soon, you'll be on your way if you commit yourself to practice and emulate behaviors required to be a solid leader.

Part of practice in action and staying focused is to quickly assess the impact of changes in any given situation. Sometimes there are organizational changes and new insights. Any of these changes dictates how you might respond or position yourself. While working on Capitol Hill, I watched members of Congress demonstrate political savvy maneuvering by quickly advocating for various issues and at the same time remaining focused on relationship-building. In this way, they often garnered support for a particular cause or issue. In the same way, I zeroed in on allies and historically common ground in my political career through specific consensus-building on key issues. Sometimes it meant closely listening to reflections from allies about an issue and then later referencing these comments to demonstrate support or endorsement of a like-minded position. In that way, I was repeatedly gathering support through deliberate political maneuvering essential to successful leadership.

 Resilience is what it takes to become a good leader.

STAY THE COURSE

Another aspect of practice is staying the course from start to finish. It is about developing a pattern or routine to achieve some objective. To have a routine is about discipline every day to a specific course of action, timeframe, or follow through. For most leaders, there is some regimen that improves their objectives or endeavors. Having repetition standardizes a leader's overall thought process and, in turn, creates a benchmark for most efforts. With my school board meeting routine, I developed a system to prepare for meetings including letting the phone ring through to voice mail, keeping work meetings and travel to a minimum, and playing inspirational music as I gathered my notes and readied myself.

One word of caution: Do not practice a haphazard routine. Otherwise, you will be defeating your purpose and learn the desired skill the wrong way. I'm amazed about how many people do the same thing over and over again only to realize they have learned something the wrong way. I'm no exception. But, over the years it takes me a shorter period of time to realize that I'm making the same mistake over again. With my school board meeting routine as an example, it took me several tries before realizing that I had to develop a systemic process to prepare for meeting discussions; otherwise, my mind was scattered. The key to a routine is to keep doing it until you get it right. Once you get the details in place, you can go from there.

 Repeated practice and tenacity will help you become a better leader.

Finally, once you get it right, practice the scenario the same in every situation. You will go through patterns. By doing this, it will move you quickly from being a newcomer to a formidable and conscientious leader. You already have many of these relevant tools for success from past roles, so dust them off and start practicing. You do not have to wait for a green light to assume the helm!

Stay Committed

While perfection is a desired outcome from ongoing practice and diligence, it is impossible. Nonetheless, there are some ways you might cultivate your abilities in your quest. One way is a commitment to learn and practice fundamentals the right way. For me, this meant identifying and working to improve the most challenging tasks experienced during my leadership capacity. What comes to mind was how I timed expressing concern about issues either during a meeting or in-person with constituents. Early in my tenure, I felt personally challenged to address policy issues or constituent concerns almost immediately. Gradually, I learned to find the most appropriate time and venue to express my concerns and reflections from constituents, sometimes in a public forum. With practice, my intended message became more effective when I addressed a specific inquiry with consideration of the impact and subsequent potential impact.

 Be committed to practice one leadership skill every day. Just remember that managing leadership skills takes time.

LEADERSHIP SECRETS

- Practice different strategies to refine your leadership approach.

- Assess your leadership strengths and weaknesses.

- Stay focused on your vision and priorities.

- Assess the landscape of every situation and make adjustments as necessary.

- Repeat actions to yield specific improvement.

CHAPTER 9:

Get Up and Keep Going

*The game called life knocks you down, beats you
up, and kicks you in the teeth. You can think
about, talk about, and be about it. But until
you do something about it, nothing counts. Don't
just sit there, get up and finish the race!*

Unplanned circumstances will derail almost anyone. But when you are in charge and leading others, the added complexity is to maintain your composure despite the unexpected. You have to find the inner resolve to keep going even when there's confusion. You must be tenacious and stay on task almost without missing a beat.

You might ask yourself: Where will I find the inner strength to keep going in the face of adversity? How can I keep my "game face" on to maintain a high level of professionalism? Here are several sustaining factors and an action plan with Leadership Building Blocks in mind to use when you might just want to throw in the towel.

ARE THOSE TIRE MARKS ON YOUR BACK?

My first year on the school board was the most challenging as I learned the district culture. It seemed our board was endlessly reviewing board protocols to guide how we would interact, a structure clearly not in place. The school district was in the middle of an unprecedented era of high school reform that resulted in the opening of more than a dozen new charter schools. It felt like I had tire marks on my backside. It almost felt like I was getting mowed down in the oncoming traffic of rapid-fire votes that might well have been pre-ordained.

To be prepared for votes and board meeting discussions, I spent endless nights getting organized and researching various policy issues. On top of that, our board passed several resolutions to close neighborhood schools in 2004 and 2005, displacing students and causing a log-jam in district student enrollment. At the same time, I often cast dissenting votes on positions and my inquisitive nature was contrary to current board culture.

Some board colleagues and constituents seemed surprised that I continued going against the grain, citing greater district accountability, equity, and efficiency as I seemingly was run down and off the road for voicing my opinion. Even as I faced criticism during a time of unexpected dynamics, daily renewal helped me stay focused on decisions that were right for me. Later, I learned that asking thorough questions helped the entire district.

These situations were further complicated by a community report circulating with allegations of conflicts of interests from 2000 by current and former board members as well as school district administrators. Constituents were angry about the apparent misappropriation of funds and blasted the entire board. The public drew negative conclusions about all politicians that did not seem fair. How was there such an egregious oversight by elected leaders and my board colleagues? Why was I being blamed for what happened before I arrived? Why were there generalizations without a chance to show that I was different? This was not what I had expected at all.

At some point in those early days, I committed to myself that I would find a way to endure uncertainty and complexity. I would provide leadership—regardless of the circumstance—for the students I served in the school district. Not only had I taken an oath of office, I had an obligation to honor my family name and, more importantly, my personal integrity.

 Be clear about your objectives during times of unexpected challenges and have an action plan. Regardless of criticism, questions, or doubts, stay focused. Otherwise, you might get bogged down and lose sight.

THIS MESSAGE WILL NOT SELF-DESTRUCT

When casting votes, some board colleagues and constituents did not understand my dissenting opinion and explanation provided. Fellow trustees did not believe our decisions required detailed rationale, if any, but that the superintendent or staff recommendation were sufficient. Yet, I stayed true to my convictions. What I needed were facts, documentation, and the potential implications before making most decisions. This went back to my graduate public policy training and years managing programs with cost-benefit analysis and benchmarks to determine effectiveness. With this in mind, I was often the only trustee requesting more information, sometimes putting a vote on hold. While I found courage to speak my convictions, a new question emerged in my effort to persevere: How was my message going to be sustained and conveyed?

After only a few initial board meetings, I realized that my requests and rationale were not being recorded or tracked by staff or the superintendent. What I offered as solutions might well have gone into a black hole. Meeting discussions were lost in cryptic board meeting minutes that stated "board discussion followed." District staff had technical challenges using video recording equipment that had endless, unexplained repairs that went on for more than a year. And on top of that, my decisions were occasionally stated without my explanation by the print media. It hurt me when the local press portrayed my decisions as the wrong choice rather than respecting philosophical differences.

Nonetheless, an essential quality for any leader is tenacity. Having the inner resolve to keep exploring alternatives will help you when dismayed by challenges. For me, the roadblocks to explain my positions taken were frustrating and discouraging but not insurmountable. If board protocols and mainstream media could not explain how a dissenting opinion was able to co-exist on the board, then I could. Instead, other venues were the new platform where I shared my rationale. First, I made an unprecedented move asking the superintendent and staff to add my bullet-point comments into the official meeting record. After a few meetings, colleagues noticed my new strategy but no one said anything. While staff was not inspired to revise how meeting minutes were recorded, that was no problem for me. The message was being delivered. During individual board member reflections at the end of each meeting, I circled back to specific comments I had made on a specific issue or vote. It was also helpful when I contacted mainstream print media to offer them a formal statement to use rather than accepting what they printed. Then I utilized alternative print media to share my positions through writing articles and opinion columns. As I found courage to get up and keep going when it seemed unbearable, I had also discovered a new voice to speak up.

 When your message is not told when and how you desire, find alternative ways to share your opinions, thoughts, and convictions. Without your input, no one will understand your decision and deliberations.

As I pressed forward, asking questions about a partially inept policymaking system with glaring loopholes, it was not until the middle of my tenure that I was somewhat vindicated. Improprieties by several board colleagues were brought forward in a grand jury investigation in 2004, including misuse of district funds and inappropriate policy decisions. Constituents rallied and mounted an immediate recall campaign against four of these board members. I escaped unscathed since all improper action happened before my arrival. Other trustees had to answer questions they were unwilling or uninterested in doing so beforehand. While I had risen above the fray, now some people realized why I asked so many questions. Some started to understand my leadership style and my courage to stand up. Many soon realized I would always get back up despite setbacks or distractions.

SPINNING NEGATIVITY

Serving in any leadership capacity means that you will eventually experience some negativity. Quite simply, it is the standard in many leadership arenas because there is a jockeying for power and control of resources. Hence the term mud-slinging might describe a process or forums where there is a push-pull factor. With this complexity, you will likely become a victim of personal verbal attacks, negative press, lies, rumors, and slanderous commentary about your person, style, or philosophical beliefs. Other times this might include a misrepresentation about how you voted or simply false information. In public service, your life is subject to inquiry and anything potentially questionable will be scrutinized and possible adversely portrayed. Either way, what will you do? How do you react?

 The key to being a successful leader who perseveres is to deal with any negative spin head on, moving around it, or spinning it in another direction. You must prepare yourself for the inevitable.

First, do not ignore negative depictions. Your silence might send a message that you concur. My recommendation is that you respond. You should first find out the source of the commentary, if possible. In turn, develop a concise response citing specifically how these are false assertions. Seek advice from your closest advisors, friends and family, or mentors. You might hold a press conference with allies flanked on either side or distribute a press announcement stating the facts. If the commentary affects other leaders, you might want to see if they will join you in a rebuttal. (We'll discuss more about communication skills in Chapter 17.) Nonetheless, hold your head high and keep moving despite any misperceptions.

In addition, you must always keep a critical eye on all that is going on. You will need to be aware of critics, opponents, and naysayers. Stay alert for changing dynamics and shifting patterns. The more prepared you are and faster action you take, it's likely that it will be easier to bounce back from the impact of anything negative. For instance, if you know potential rumors might circulate after a specific event, vote, or leadership discussion, you can be ready.

 Proceed carefully when responding to inquiries. There is nothing worse than off-the-cuff remarks or unintended outcomes from a live microphone.

LEADERSHIP SECRETS

- Stay focused despite criticism and uncertainty.

- Find your inner strength and creativity to share your message and convictions.

- Be prepared to meet critics and opponents.

- Deal with negativity on a case-by-case basis, developing a solid response. Stay alert of changing dynamics to provide clues.

- Face external and internal challenges head on.

PART 4

DYNAMIC CREATIVITY

Bringing innovative perspectives to your leadership position is essential. In Part Four, we explore the fourth Leadership Building Block that encourages you to bring creativity to your leadership role. In Chapter 10, we review the significance of getting organized. What does it take to get set up? How do you learn the lay of the land and organizational protocols? In Chapter 11, highlights about creative time management strategies are discussed.

CHAPTER 10:

Game Time—Get Organized!

"You can show up in life any way you want.
You just have to decide how you want to show up."

—*Anonymous*

During the first few months in your new position, you will get acclimated in several ways. You are getting yourself established and likewise learning your role along with industry acronyms and legalese. At the same time, you have to get organized and learn to manage numerous new business and community relationships. It's a virtual frenzy as you listen to system jargon for weeks or even months, almost like searching for answers in vegetable soup! Some business guides suggest it takes about 100 days for leaders to get up and running. One of the most exciting parts of getting acclimated in the political maze was maneuvering through the system while the political process keeps moving. There were weekly information packets, briefs and protocols, strategic plans, and constituent inquiries for me to read.

Similarly, in your leadership role you will have an opportunity to showcase your multi-tasking capability by juggling priorities. Keeping in mind Leadership Building Blocks, let's talk about meeting preparation and getting yourself set up and ready for game time.

LEARN THE BASICS

To get yourself established, your first objective is to learn the system. It is more than learning your way around buildings and how to set up filing systems. As with any organization, there are written and implicit rules. You will need to learn the time commitments, legal obligations, and mandated requirements. This may require careful planning and outlining all the issues to be addressed. Some are explicit, others are implied.

Who's On First?

First steps first: You must find out who will help you. Determine who on staff is available to assist you with administrative duties—mail processing, constituent follow up, committee meeting preparation, and conference logistics. This may include several staff members and/or one individual assigned to assist a leadership team. It was eye-opening to learn one person supported the seven-member school board with weekly meeting preparation. That was remarkable! Shared support is different than a personal secretary or team to help with assignments. As one of the nation's top fifty largest school districts, to have minimal board support was surprising.

To get acclimated, set up one-on-one meetings with this gatekeeper and others. This will help you get situated. These people will be your best resource and keep an eye out for your issues and projects of interest. Survey your colleagues and mentors to learn what works for them.

Home Base

Developing an office structure and filing system is vital. On a regular basis, constituents called me for information and opinions. To be prepared, you need to be organized and ready to respond. While you are not expected to have immediate answers, having an organized filing system will help make sure you grasp issues and organizational materials quickly. Be sure you are ready with answers to respond in a timely, courteous way.

First, you will need to set up your home office with basic office essentials including computer equipment, printer, a fax machine, recycle bin, and general office supplies. Keep in mind that the organization you work for may have a work station. In my case, this was a shared public work station. Even though you may have an office or office space within your jurisdiction, you will want to make sure you have a system at home to respond to inquiries.

Second, install a dedicated telephone line separate from your home telephone line. In my case, the school board was considering contentious issues that resulted in my telephone answering machine staying full for weeks on end. Soon thereafter, I had a second telephone line installed at home—one dedicated for public service business and another for personal calls.

Third, invest in a filing cabinet and lockbox to categorize information and secure sensitive materials. I transformed the closet of my home office into "public service central" with an in-box sorter file for constituent inquiries. In the file cabinet that fit into the closet were files about board protocols, committee assignments, and staff rosters. With files readily available, I quickly responded to constituent inquiries.

 Get set up to manage the weekly "paper trail" that finds its way into your office. Bring your creative ideas to develop a system that works for you.

Who's Minding the Shop?

With Leadership Building Blocks, it's essential to understand organizational norms and unstated organizational culture. Some questions you might ask: Who holds the power—staff or leadership? How does the system function? What is the process of requesting information from staff? Who does what and how can you learn more? Sometimes these questions are answered in any formal orientation, but more often you will learn it over time.

First, you might get better acquainted by conducting informational interviews—informal one-on-one discussions with staff, community-based organizations, and colleagues. With this, you learn who does what and where to get more information.

Next, understand the leadership team configurations and where the base of power rests. On the school board, the superintendent had authority for day-to-day operations and staff oversight. Board members collectively governed policy issues and directed the superintendent. Be clear about your authority and role on the leadership team. Knowing how to garner allies is another essential role. You will need to check with the experts on various topics of interest and, in some instances, staff and gatekeepers who have wielded power.

Furthermore, what I needed to know was the process for getting issues on the meeting agenda, changing policy, and the committee assignment process. I learned that our board executive committee had three members with elevated authority to set meeting agendas. The executive committee changed and deleted any issues for consideration. Keep in mind how to get your issues on the agenda and up for discussion.

SOCIAL ETIQUETTE

What resources are available to you? First, be aware of your social interaction skills. Interacting with people from different cultures, ethnic groups, and socioeconomic backgrounds each week requires solid communication skills. How well do you pick up on the motivation of others? Are you savvy about socially appropriate communication? Cues from your constituency and colleagues will give you further insight. Many of my constituents were more than curious how I became comfortable speaking in front of large audiences and conversant with people of different economic and social backgrounds. Raised in the San Francisco Bay area, I had, on more than one occasion, dealt with people from different social strata. Community service roles in the church and soup kitchens, and then on Capitol Hill also blended my interactions. The opportunities I had at youth centers, senior health facilities, and college preparation centers taught the importance of dealing with different people. I learned to meet people "where they were" in their respective venues.

Not only is it important to take a look at your personal and social interactions but also your ability to deal with different situations. In your leadership role, attending social events will become part of your daily routine, so you will likely need to become comfortable in different venues. These include black tie affairs, dinner banquets, community meetings, ethnic celebrations, informal gatherings, and faith-based events. Ask yourself some key questions: What background do you have with handling yourself in different social situations? If you have none, is there someone who can help you learn?

Draw upon your prior leadership experiences and community-based and professional roles to become more astute handling different situations and events.

Furthermore, remain attentive to your attire, public comments you might be asked to make, and how to interact with various groups. Years of attending similar events in my professional governmental relations career and church community had prepared me for dealing with both types of events—the pomp and circumstance and casual come-as-you-are. Remember, as a leader in a public role, you will need to be aware of the expectations for conducting yourself at a formal banquet (including using the appropriate utensils) as well as at receptions or outdoor gatherings.

 Do your homework to learn appropriate protocol for any occasion.

As a leader, you will be judged by your appearance and upkeep wherever you go. Without knowing, your clothes, hairstyle, color schemes, and personal style create an image and send a message. You should know the basics about appropriate professional attire; know that your image speaks volumes to your character. If you previously ran to the grocery store or the local gym without looking your best in a sweat suit and a baseball cap, you will want to reconsider. Just be conscientious about how you suit up if you prefer not to draw unnecessary attention to yourself.

Finally, be prudent and take etiquette cues from your colleagues or get insight from mentors. Get some helpful "tricks of the trade" about successfully working a room. By now, you should be over the fear of meeting new people and be able to extend a smile and a handshake to a stranger. Just in case, call upon all the courage you can muster to get beyond your comfort zone. If you serve in any average-size, high-profile position, this could mean hundreds or thousands of interactions within any given week. You may want a colleague to accompany you if this is an unfamiliar audience. Be mindful of expectations that you stay awhile to schmooze and engage in light banter or chit-chat. Also, do a little homework beforehand to learn more about the organization, event, and leadership for the event you'll attend. The slightest familiarity will be invaluable. Finally, get the "heads up" about arriving late and leaving early. Be prepared to excuse your tardiness or early departure. Be gracious at the event and afterwards.

Weekly Round Up

On a weekly basis, you will receive updates, announcements, sometimes significant mail to review. Schedule yourself to attend community events. In my case, there was no secretary to open and review mail or schedule and print my weekly calendar. That was my administrative duty in addition to reviewing board meeting materials for weekly board meetings.

Suiting Up

Depending on the size, type, and magnitude of issues you will encounter, you will have a variety of expectations to guide your meeting preparation. Typically, your meeting materials should be provided well in advance of each meeting. Realistically, this will be a week beforehand for you to read materials, ask staff questions, and develop positions for expected votes. In my case, the bi-weekly board packet arrived sporadically from the beginning of my tenure. Sometimes, last-minute revisions or new information was added the night before the meeting. Even when I arrived at the meeting, there was often a colorful stack of documents stamped "revised" that required a quick read before a vote. Last-minute materials presented by staff called for board approval on financial, academic programs, and systemic considerations. This was unacceptable. The lack of due diligence hampered reasonable decision-making and my concerns were registered on this issue on more than one occasion.

Come to meetings as if you are ready for a classroom lesson. I brought several tools—ballpoint pens, colored highlighters, and tab and paper post-it notes—to quickly help with review of any information. This also helped facilitate my pointed questions. Asking questions and drawing attention to an issue mentioned on slide twelve of fifty in a 20-minute slide presentation was simplified with the proper tools. What was also helpful was to review my notes afterwards just in case I needed additional information or to reiterate concerns on an issue. You'll be a star player if you do the same. It's best to be prepared for anything in meetings. That could range from the unexpected from administrative staff or information shared by the public.

GAME TIME—MEETING CONVENED

Come prepared to each meeting with materials read and a series of questions. You have an obligation to your constituents to review all possible angles of any issue before voting. I developed a routine prior to each meeting to forward the superintendent a list of questions to discuss specific agenda items. Most memorable is a list of fifteen questions I emailed to the superintendent regarding the forthcoming vote on the closure of Sacramento High School. When we spoke, he was astonished that I had so many questions.

As a steward of the public trust, it seemed to be due diligence to understand the rationale and impact of the decision. I wanted to know about documentation justifying the school closure and conversion, any potential for a lawsuit if the board approved closing the school, and what would happen to the students displaced by the closure. He refused to provide answers to my questions. Just a few weeks later, my name, referenced as "an earnest freshman board member," and a compelling question appeared in an article about Sacramento High School on the front page of the January 27, 2003, *Sacramento Bee* that read: "Do we have to close the school to consider a charter school?" I had no idea at the time about the significance of the question I asked. Only now looking back, I see what happened: I had prepared and asked questions calling for perpetual board accountability of protocols, policymaking, financial obligations, due diligence, and public accountability. The thousands who gathered in a public outcry and a split board made a difference. It became the mantra and a call-and-response between me and like-minded constituents. It resulted in almost four years of continuous debate about the closure and unintended implications: displaced parents and district teachers and staff, dismantled college preparation programs, disgruntled parents, strained teachers union-school district relations, lawsuit by parents, board member recall campaign, judicial mandate, public outcry and disenchantment, grand jury investigation, and conflicts of interest.

GET OUT THE PLAY BOOK

Become well-versed in parliamentary procedure and memorize protocols for conducting public business. When I started serving, there were no rules to guide our public discourse and interaction. Regularly, colleagues turned off my microphone or talked over me while I tried to make a point where we disagreed. Sometimes during heated discussions, opposing colleagues tag-teamed me and pressed me for a vote. With dog-eared, war-torn pages of the school board protocols I gently and repeatedly reminded colleagues and staff that I knew the rules. And keep in mind that in politics, rules are subject to change. One day it was alright for seasoned board members to roam the audience during meetings and another day I was being scolded for leaving the dais to stretch and get fresh air during marathon five-hour meetings. Above all, remember the rules but also keep in mind you are helping your constituents learn the rules. You are encouraging them to abide by these principles for public discourse. (We'll talk about teaching others through your example in Chapter 14.)

CONFERENCES AND TRAINING

To refine your skills, get adequate training. Your colleagues or chief administrator can recommend industry conferences you should attend. You will discover useful resources to assist you with your learning process and professional development. Some essential skills include conducting business, advocacy, teamwork, and self-evaluation. Trainings provided by state and local industry associations and businesses will provide helpful insight to help you become a more effective leader. As a leader, you can stay informed and learn the latest techniques and trends that will affect your jurisdiction. Here is a list of some effective conference networking tips:

- Establish networking goals.
- Learn about committees and conference sessions of interest in conference programs.

- Explore a "Beginner" track to get better acquainted with the industry you serve.
- Use networking with mentors and colleagues to meet new people.
- Develop a concise self-introduction about yourself and services provided.
- Use business cards, a notebook, and calendar to set up meetings and follow-up.
- Set reasonable goals to stay connected at receptions, meal functions, and the exhibit area.
- Coordinate conference sessions and functions to attend with colleagues.
- Be a resource offering your expertise to conference/industry committees and workshops.

LEADERSHIP SECRETS

- Get yourself organized with logistics and resources.
- Master team dynamics, organizational norms, and expectations.
- Gauge your social etiquette knowledge and prepare accordingly.
- Make regular appearances at events and trainings based on your interests and expectations.
- Prepare before meetings and discussions by learning appropriate rules and protocols.

CHAPTER 11:

Runners, Take Your Mark!

Managing your time wisely will go miles in the long run.

You're probably thinking to yourself that there does not seem to be that much involved with being a leader. Quite the opposite! Demands and expectations of your leadership position will pull you away from your personal life and your regular full-time job. Before you can get started in your new role, all your electronic inboxes—email, voice message, and fax machine—are blinking "You've got mail" and you have binders, reports, and summaries to read daily before the next formal meeting. In fact, your leadership role might feel like a second job.

As a school board trustee, I reviewed education materials, attended community meetings, and responded to inquiries from hundreds of constituents each week. Inquiries racked up through public comment at meetings and snail mail was delivered to my home. I also wanted to attend regular family gatherings and outings with friends and meet travel and workplace expectations for my full-time job working with college and university financial aid administrators. At that time, I only carved out a marginal part of my everyday schedule for self-care. Finally, after struggling to do it all for a few weeks I had enough sense to know that a time management system was needed. I had to prioritize demands competing for my time. If I was going to be successful as a leader, I had to step up and get my act together! In this chapter, you will learn more about using and tracking your time wisely, an aspect of the Leadership Building Blocks that will help you set reasonable expectations for yourself.

On Your Mark!

In track and field, a sprinter prepares carefully before getting into the starting blocks. Careful precision is necessary and this detail includes the athletes measuring steps and placing the starting block accordingly. This gives the athlete full advantage of a strong start. The objective is to virtually fly out of the blocks bursting into speed to win the race. Prior to getting in the starting blocks, sprinters also take note of weather conditions and race dynamics to adjusting their strategy. Take it from me since I was a highly-ranked competitive sprinter in high school.

Since you gained clarity about your objectives and vision in Chapter 3, you will need to control your workload and as many extraneous influences as possible. To do this, you must manage your time and obligations—personal, professional, and your leadership role. Time management can be defined as the ability to manage simultaneous priorities in a systemic fashion to accomplish specific goals. Some people assume that time management just happens. On the contrary, it requires consistent discipline and using your time effectively. First, set priorities and parameters about how you allocate your time in support of your primary objectives. For me, my time and corresponding activities were allocated to personal care and health, family, work, and community.

Get Set!

Getting into the starting blocks is all about getting ready. To be prepared, you must have a solid understanding about specific goals you aim to accomplish, meeting dates, and the time commitments associated with your new role. For example, are you expected to serve on subcommittees or other obligations? Are there other duties and community events you will be required to attend, including sub-committee meetings, special events, annual ceremonies and holiday gatherings? What about a contingency plan when meetings go later than expected?

Next, develop a paper or electronic calendar system to manage personal and professional activities. A personal digital assistant (PDA) will distinguish color-coding for work activities, family, social, and community events. To manage your constituent correspondence you will need to maximize coffee appointments, lunches, and dinners. Your time is precious so be clear about how much time you will devote to correspondence and meetings. With a solid scheduling system such as the following, your participation can be easily managed.

- Email/Telephone/Referral
- Close-ended (coffee/lunch meetings)
- Open-ended (dinner banquet, gala celebrations, etc.)

 Get organized and be proactive.

Finally, you must develop a system to resolve personal and professional schedule conflicts. What will be your benchmark criteria favoring one event rather than another? Will you attend the family event planned months ago or go to the emergency board meeting called a few hours ago? Will you skip work to attend a press conference? The fact is this: You will need to gracefully decline invitations and be selective about attending most activities. There is just not enough time for one person to attend everything.

For me, there were several determining factors, including my livelihood and the oath I had taken to act, vote, and serve thousands of Sacramento residents. To be honest, however, the bottom line was simple: working full-time was my primary objective as a sole breadwinner. If I did not work, I did not eat. With official meetings, I scheduled and committed myself to as many as possible where they did not conflict with travel expectations for my job.

What became a challenge was when school district staff added or changed scheduled meeting times on short notice and when consideration of several contentious issues required more frequent board discussions. Interestingly enough, there were requests from civic associations, other elected officials, and constituents to attend community events scattered throughout the day and week. These events really had me deliberating between personal care, family time, dinner banquets, weekend picnic celebrations, or lunch hour ceremonies.

To fulfill as many obligations as I could, I created side-by-side columns listing the advantages and drawbacks of attending one event or another. That way, I could acknowledge to myself and possibly others whatever decision seemed most logical. Tradeoffs were imperative. Without attention to time management, you will be pulled in different directions and likely get off track from your goals.

 Focus on details to be prepared and organized.

Within a few weeks of assuming your new role, you are off and running in the leadership maze. But before you jump in, get some logistics in order. Consult some seasoned veterans in your arena about what they did to get organized. You may need to delegate assignments to staff.

Next, you will want to inform family and friends about forthcoming orientations and meetings. You will have a list of last-minutes additions to your calendar to balance along with your full-time work schedule, family commitments, and personal obligations. Your personal calendar will be impacted, but use what you've learned to get yourself prepared accordingly.

Go!

In turn, you will need to set up a process to stay on goal to handle administrative tasks and to read and respond to constituent mail and email. This is similar to when a sprinter comes out of the starting blocks. How will you process and respond to these inquiries? I chose to respond before and after work to email inquiries. Over the weekend, I read letters from students and parents. Other inquiries were either referred to staff, the superintendent, or responded to with a handwritten thank you note.

 Log pending issues and telephone calls into a notebook. Regularly review your schedule.

To stay on goal and task, there are two methods I initiated. First, I completed an assessment of goals I hoped to accomplish, which I updated every three months. In line with that, I created a weekly task sheet for myself divided by constituency and policy issue. Both forms helped me remain clear about priorities and make appropriate adjustments, as necessary. Through this process I stayed focused on goals I set out to accomplish and tasks required for effective leadership such as time-sensitive telephone calls, emails or thank you notes to follow up on, or preparation for the following week. A copy of the goals framework is included in Appendix A: Leadership Building Blocks Template.

Finally, you will need an office-on-wheels. Seriously! Running between events, meetings, family gatherings, and work commitments, grabbing meals on the go and returning calls makes for long days. More often than not, I also needed to freshen up before a meeting or change into sneakers to get in a quick walk as part of a fragmented exercise routine. Keep an extra pair of shoes, bottled water, and dried fruit or granola snacks handy. Also, use a portable sorting file to transport key files. Think about what works for you.

You should also learn to maximize downtime while waiting for meetings to begin, between meetings, and during long travel times. All were prime time for me to catch up on reading periodicals, returning telephone calls, and reviewing weekly tasks.

LEADERSHIP SECRETS

- Be attentive to time management among personal, professional, and your leadership role.

- Commit yourself to a system on paper or electronically to manage leadership obligations.

- Weigh the pros and cons of attending events, activities, or duty beyond your assigned post.

- Evaluate how your schedule supports your leadership goals.

PART 5

EVERYTHING IS GLOBAL

Coalition-building is an essential part of effective leadership. It means having a global perspective. In Part Five, we explore what it takes to become a successful leader. In Chapters 12 and 13, we review the significance of relationship-building and forming a personal circle of allies. Where will you find support when you are trying to develop the Leadership Building Blocks principles? How will you distinguish between friends, acquaintances, and "frenemies"? More importantly, we will review how to develop and maintain your network. Pitfalls to avoid and lessons to learn are highlighted. Finally, as a leader, you have an obligation to mentor other rising leaders. Mentoring is discussed in Chapter 14.

CHAPTER 12:
Can We Be Friends?

"Friends are those who nourish your spirit."

—*Anonymous*

Accept this truth: As a leader you will keep some friends and also lose allies. You have reason to be excited over the prospect of gaining many new friends. But, do not be surprised if along the way you make several new enemies too. The reasons might be real or perceived and might be based on disclosed or unknown reasons. As you ascend to the leadership circle, you will need to quickly assess the difference between your friends and foes. In this chapter, you will learn about another one of the Leadership Building Blocks—how to define your base of support, fair-weather friends, and hero worshippers, and how to deal with unexpected relationship perils along the way.

As a leader, you will come to understand that the term "friend" describes a broad category—real friends, casual acquaintances, professional colleagues, and political allies. Genuine friendship exists but frequently outside of the circles of where business is conducted. I found in politics that everything is somewhat skewed and superficial and that most of my dealings were with casual acquaintances and colleagues. It's not that friendship could not be cultivated but serving in a leadership roles does not always allow you to develop trust.

Friends are those who will be your advocate on a case-by-case or regular basis. These are the people who will help you maneuver through murky waters in your leadership journey. A few allies might even swim with you a good distance. For me, these included those who were my long-time friends, campaign supporters, and professional colleagues who respected me before political celebrity status.

Got Friends?

You've heard the phrase, "Keep your friends close and your enemies even closer." This is most evident in a high-ranking leadership position. Developing relationships takes time and in leadership roles, time marches to a faster beat. In short, you do not have time on your side to develop long-standing relationships but rather you will be required to act fast on various decisions. As a result, you will have to accept that sometimes leadership is a lonely business. With this reality in mind, understand that you will only have a handful of real, trustworthy friends. Why? People have a different focus. As a transplant to Sacramento, I learned that most constituents had long-standing relationships with each other before my arrival that precluded me from having the same rapport.

To help you stay balanced, focus on reinforcing friendships with those who knew you before your new public role. Long-term friends have a deeper investment with you and will likely remain a significant presence in your life, friends you connected with before your high-profile position and who know your quirks and vulnerabilities and accept you without judgment. These are also the people who will listen without a need to reconstruct discussions from a public forum or news report. You can still develop new friendships. But any new ties established after you take the reins may come with strings attached.

As a leader, you will learn quickly who to include in your circle of trusted advisors and who to avoid. While your circle includes friends, advisors, and family members who have earned and built loyalty over a period of time, new perceived allies are either recommended or screened and may join your journey. But all that glitters is not gold. I learned the hard way that I had to secure my base and confirm loyalty when my personal information floated in the public domain. It was not that I did not want people to know everything about me, but I did want to maintain some sense of privacy. I learned to float my own rumors within my own circle of friends to learn who and what might be shared. While it might appear that I undermined my base, I concluded that I had to confirm my support.

Who's on Home Base?

In any leadership role, maintain your base of supporters. These are the folks who will praise you and be your advocates along the way. For a political leader or candidate, these are constituents. For an administrator or corporate leader, these are a variety of loyal staff and other colleagues. Always reconnect with your primary supporters and those who stand by you: friends, co-workers, voters, advocates, volunteers, party affiliates, and community organizations.

Your base is drawn to you for a variety of reasons that might include your platform, your values, or perspectives. Draw upon their support as you implement your vision and goals. As the "product" endorsed through an election, nomination, or appointment, you are expected to fulfill promises to your base, further reinforcing their support and, in turn, likely their circles of friends. I made it a point to fulfill campaign expectations and to bring in new supporters with volunteer sign-up forms and one-page information sheets.

Not surprising, some will support you on a single issue. Accept that single-issue friends will love you today and will hate you tomorrow. Their fondness for you may come and go depending on your weekly voting record or other public discussions or positions taken. For me, this meant that these constituents would support me on a specific issue or over a limited timeframe. Regardless, they still remain within my base of support. Simply accept the ebb and flow of their support.

To further secure your base, maintain open and frequent communication. You might develop and send a newsletter and also address core issues in public forums and meetings. You will want to follow up when a constituent has an inquiry. (More about support through community engagement is discussed in Chapter 13.)

 Set up regular meetings with advocates and organizations to maintain their support for your endeavors.

Fair-weather Friends

You'll soon discover that you have a group of friends who are here today and gone tomorrow. Fair-weather friends are those who sway in their support for you. You might see this support waning or it just might happen without notice. These folks can turn on you in a New York minute! A change in the winds of fair-weather friendships might be based on an issue, decision, position taken, or time of day. These might be people envious of your small wins, suspicious of your intentions, or who might have a real dislike for you. For me, these were those who were fond of me and then who chided me publicly or behind my back for decisions made. Working in the political arena for more than a decade, I have come to recognize those who purport to be a friend are more likely an evolving foe. Tell-tale signs are a lack of loyalty and no steadfast commitment to you and your causes.

By the same token, some will offer a helping hand but not without a potential price tag or favor in return. For example, are they just friends with you to accomplish their own personal gain such as a job, business opportunity, or stone-stepping opportunity? Are they power-mongers just trying to motivate themselves? Be wary. With someone only looking out for their own personal objectives behind the scenes, do you really need friends like this? Just say no!

On the contrary, be aware of these so-called friends who leave you to fend for yourself when times get tough. Genuine friends will stand by you. However, fair-weather friends will sway in their allegiance between you and others. This might be to gain some access to real or perceived power. You will read more about how to chart dangerous territory in Chapter 15, so keep your eyes open for these "friends."

A fair-weather friend might pledge support but will not stand by to support you during crunch time.

Hero Worship: Who Loves You?

As a leader, you will have hero worshippers. These include friends and acquaintances alike who will worship you for what you stand for and positions you take. Some are those enamored by you, your star-like beginnings, or power that your position exudes. As a new political leader, I was flattered to have support for votes I cast. But I was not foolish enough to take the bait and accept the celebrity status so many politicians accept from overzealous advocates. It's great to have loyal supporters and a fan club, but only if it comes with honest motives and if it is sustained. Otherwise, these are simply fair-weather friends.

During my school board days, I had a constituent who turned out to be an admirer who asked to meet with me under the guise of talking politics and general education issues. Somewhere during the meeting, he shared his real motive: he was an admirer and had romantic inklings in mind. He actually said that he just wanted to sit and stare at me in person. What leader has time for this? What woman leader who has worked so hard to accomplish a level of respect, authority, and power only to be called upon by an admirer and informed that she's now a beauty pageant finalist, would be pleased by this? Not exactly my most flattering moment. But it was very insightful and a reminder about how different people have different reasons for supporting leaders. Certainly I accepted the compliment about my beauty but remained focused on my core agenda, knowing that I could not be effective with "pop star" status.

Be gracious with hero worshippers, but stay focused on your leadership agenda. Consider clarifying for yourself where hero worshippers fit in either as authentic friends and your base of support category or as a fair-weather friend or potential foe. It's better to determine if their admiration is about you or about something else.

The Social Scene

You will also be scrutinized by who you associate with, why you are with them, and where you are. Do you remember your mother saying, "You are the company you keep"? It will be even more important now that you are a leader. Since you want people to see you as honest, reliable, knowledgeable, and professional, you will need to have corresponding actions, behaviors, and associations. In your new role, you will be scrutinized whenever you're in the public eye. Be mindful since those you serve will be quick to judge and slow to forgive.

If you are single, you will want to be very discreet about your dating life. How does who you are dating help people understand your decision-making as a leader? That's right, it does not. Thus, it is nobody's business who and if you are dating. Unfortunately, sometimes people do not know how to handle the privacy of a leader. Sometimes it might appear that people want to know relationships you have had in order to better understand who you are and what makes you tick. It's best to be cordial but keep your personal matters private.

LIONS AND TIGERS AND BEARS—OH MY!

Along your journey you will find another interesting type who I call "frenemies"—just a step beyond authentic enemies. What makes these people so unique is that they are critics and opponents who mask themselves under the guise of a false friendship. These malicious types will hurt you through verbal attacks, insults, and deceit. Sometimes they might persuade others to turn their backs on you to intentionally hurt you. If there was a theme song, it might be the classic by the O'Jays entitled "The Backstabbers," because these people will smile in your face but you never see what is coming at you from behind. You never know when these friends might turn, share confidential conversations, or drag your good name through the mud. How can you come to identify these players? What should you do when you encounter them?

Frenemies are often not identifiable critics because they can be wolves dressed in sheep's clothing. Sometimes they announce themselves and make it known that they dislike you or what you stand for and represent. Disdain might be based on who you are or because these people are enemies of your political friends. Other times, you will have to discover frenemies over time since they will not raise their hands and announce their presence. For me, this was the reality of politics, even before I took office. Being an underdog candidate, people were more than curious about where I came from and what I stood for in my political philosophy and values. On the campaign trail and even as I got started in my new role, I had to find out who my base of supporters really was. Unbeknownst to my alleged friends—and later frenemies—I started to float my own rumors. Before long, the "telephone game" was played out and the word I put into the political arena and local political grapevine got back to me. Sure enough, I figured out the weakest links and adjusted who I shared information with on more than one occasion.

 Be wary of frenemies who purport to have your best interest. You are better suited to assess their loyalty before sharing too much.

Regardless, you must learn how to readily identify your frenemies. From my encounters, those purporting to be friends repeatedly convey half-truths, waffle in their support of you, hedge or hesitate when talking with you, and often demonstrate clear body language signals. Obvious behavioral changes include lacking, rapid, or poor eye contact and stuttering or tripping over words. One man had a great ongoing rapport with me on various education issues then he developed a perpetual eye twitch when we discussed this one particular issue. Soon I realized that I could no longer count him among my base of support; he had shifted camps and supported one of my definite opponents.

An indicator that your friendship is in trouble is when he or she is unresponsive to your correspondence, unavailable to talk or meet with you, or he or she is keeping company and public appearance with different groups that conflict with your values and positions. On another more painful occasion, a mentor who I deeply admired stopped returning my calls. Soon I received word that there was no time to be of support or time in the schedule to meet with me. Calls were returned but the conversations were aloof. I could no longer define any of these friendships as just fair-weather, but rather the official "on the fence" status of frenemies. My advice: Watch for various signals and notice everything!

Be aware of various signs that indicate your friends might not be as authentic as once imagined. Approach these situations with caution.

How will you handle what you learn once frenemies show their true colors? To manage these types of people, take stock of every incident with all suspected frenemies. Pay attention to which camps they are associated. These clues will help you understand potential intent, marching orders, power-broker style, and allegiance. It's best to avoid unnecessary confrontations with these friends of your enemies and enemies of your friends. You may even consider distinguishing some with questionable allegiance as either friends or foes but never include them in both categories. Hopefully this will force their hand so you can stay focused on your objectives.

LEADERSHIP SECRETS

- Group friends including allies, trusted advisors, family, and long-standing colleagues.

- Identify your base of supporters, whether on a single issue or several.

- Closely monitor potentially questionable support that might undermine your efforts.

- Clarify those who are your genuine advocates and those who are "frenemies."

CHAPTER 13:

Connect the Dots

There has to be more than just someone standing at the helm. Being a leader must be about moving others to action and building a sense of community.

As a leader, building alliances and coalitions is essential. To gain support for your cause or position and to be an effective leader exerting influence requires first reinforcing relationships with colleagues, clients, and constituents. Sustaining this rapport under the parameters of Leadership Building Blocks can be accomplished through advocacy, demonstrative leadership, and staying engaged in community discussions.

Solid leadership is also about exerting influence, the art of moving others to some action or outcome. In the *21 Irrefutable Laws of Leadership*, John Maxwell sums up his definition of leadership as "leadership is influence—nothing more, nothing less." This definition assesses the ability of leaders to influence others. Inherent in that definition is the presumption that leadership includes maintaining integrity, a fundamental essential to reinforce a leader's ability to influence others. In turn, following Leadership Building Blocks demonstrates that you are a leader sensitive to reinforcing multiple networks and being able to read people and situations.

Furthermore, serving as an advocate establishes mutual understanding, builds trust, and reinforces alliances. A closer look at how to be an advocate means considering essential components as blocks, or alliances, with the constituents you serve. Let's examine the definition of advocate, community, and how to effectively manage multiple networks and connect the dots.

To Advocate or Not to Advocate

Serving as an advocate means being a champion for a specific cause. It involves supporting a cause, purpose, issue, or principle. Different aspects of issues are expressed as viewpoints, opinions, or concerns. Throughout the process, an opinion is developed from various resources and perspectives. This means that your decision-making will likely be determined by multiple factors.

Serving on a school board meant I was a proactive champion for policies and effective governance while trying to stay focused without getting sidetracked. In my case, I vociferously advocated for sustained school library support when challenging fiscal constraints led school district staff to recommend elimination of school libraries and staff. It shocked me that coveted valuable learning resources were on the chopping block. I researched how staff came to this conclusion, viable cost-saving alternatives, and rationale provided by staff for the school library eliminations. Furthermore, I identified opportunity costs for students attending schools that might no longer have school libraries. After listening to students and parents, librarians, and others, I cast dissenting votes.

Given the dynamics of jockeying for scarce resources, there are perpetual situations to advocate for a specific cause, policy, or position. To accomplish this requires exerting influence and giving persuasive arguments.

As an advocate, you will address issues and implications and offer possible solutions. In the public sector, I served as an advocate at public meetings and neighborhood forums. After listening to constituent concerns, I advocated for specific education policy issues such as library funding, additional school supplies, and teacher training programs. Most of the issues were closely aligned with my leadership role priorities.

 You will engage your constituents beyond formal correspondence by responding to complaints and questions. This will help you gain public confidence and establish mutual trust.

A leader serving as an advocate will factor in perspectives from others. You are the voice of the people or cause you represent. To be effective, you must consider opinions different from your own that will demonstrate impartial decision-making. More importantly, you will be thoughtful of those you represent. Advocates sometimes—but not always—factor in recommendations from others where private organizations and individuals do not have this obligation. Votes I cast were often decisions made factoring in the opinions of others—constituents, the superintendent and staff, and board colleagues. If you are an advocate, how do you identify those in agreement or in opposition to a cause or issue?

WILL THE COMMUNITY PLEASE JOIN HANDS?

A community can be defined as a group of individuals or organizations assembled formally or by default for an intended purpose. Typically this includes people working collaboratively but who might be different ethnically, economically, socially, or politically. So how and why do communities work together? How are their concerns voiced in a forum?

First, input is provided through community dialogues to address a specific concern, inquiry, or initiative. In local politics, this included town hall meetings, breakfast forums, and neighborhood association meetings. At these discussions, issues specific to a geographic region or constituency are highlighted and shared. With school library closures, for instance, parents, students, and librarians rallied together to advocate as library supporters despite political, geographic, and ethnic differences. More specifically, advocates reinforce their strategic support by providing meeting commentary and participating in community-based dialogues and advisories.

Second, opinions are shared through formal committee or board discussions known as a comment or discussion period. During public proceedings, constituents voiced concerns in a two-minute timeframe on scheduled agenda items and a public comment period. With this limitation, however, there were perpetual misunderstandings since our board often sat stone-faced with no response. California open meeting law barred us from engaging in discussion on issues not on the agenda.

Thus, the speaker was rarely acknowledged before the next person was called to the dais. Sometimes announcements or accolades were shared. More often than not these were heartbreaking testimonies about cited lacking resources, overlooked school system accountability, or student altercations. If public input was noted, it was addressed at the discretion of the superintendent. To me, this seemed disrespectful since constituents sometimes shared a concern only to be ignored. It occurred to me that our board should do something; through board retreat discussions, eventually our district superintendent agreed. With thorough public engagement protocols, a general statement was provided informing the public that even without the board responding at that time, that all comments were tracked and responded to along with an update for the board.

Third, coalition-building is another essential process where groups work collaboratively. In this instance, these collective groups leverage each other's support for a common purpose. It is sometimes a diverse gathering of individuals or organizations to solve a problem. Why is this so important for leaders? Building a strategic alliance reinforces power and influence when defending an interest. With an established coalition, the goal is to work together, pooling resources to counter opposition or advance a position.

Finally, community advisory boards serve as a voice representing a geographic organization or constituency. Sometimes this might be topic-specific, time-sensitive, or an ongoing initiative. For the school district, there were various ethnic-based advisory boards for Asian-American, Hispanic, and African-American children that provided input on strategies to improve student academic performance and college attendance rates, among other issues. Membership included noted organization leaders. The significant role for a leader is to assess meaningful involvement and the expected outcomes. Is there a targeted duration, purpose, or finding that will result? In one situation, district staff established the "Seven-Eleven Committee" to analyze the merits of anywhere from seven to eleven elementary school closures in light of district budget constraints and declining enrollment. Yet, despite my requests for measurable feedback and meaningful community input, the staff moved forward, ignoring final committee recommendations for more thorough inquiry about implications from neighborhood school closures. Staff negligence sent shockwaves through Sacramento since input from parents, labor leaders, and community activists invited to the committee was dismissed. In another instance, a facilities committee provided documentation about overpayment and malfunctioning of school site heating and air units. Even after recommendations were made calling for the governing board to make improvements to achieve greater efficiency, the committee suggestions fell on deaf ears. In short, a leader must be astute to decipher group objectives and ensure that outcomes are measurable.

 Within each forum, leaders must stay well-informed and maneuver through the apparent on masked viewpoints to understand the organizational dynamics and objectives.

We Have Lift-Off!

After I joined the board, I noticed different interpretations about how to achieve authentic community engagement with clients, constituents, or memberships. On a public board and other similar non-profit organizations, for example, this feedback is the backbone of the organizational structure. But since my first official meeting, several board decisions were made without input from the public. My concern was simple: How does a leader assess effective engagement and go about improving it? To help find solutions, I defined for myself three categories of community engagement as authentic input, consideration of recommendations, and accountability.

First, community engagement requires authentic input where opinions are valued. Leaders take into consideration feedback from others besides themselves. On the Sacramento board; however, suggestions from the public often were not included in the decision-making process. Community input was sporadically received about issues such as allocation of resources, staff accountability, and district-wide equity. In fact, a study conducted by the Annenberg Institute in 2004 concluded that the Sacramento School District lacked adequate public engagement. The report cited that parent and community groups were not invited to weigh in on the impact of various board resolutions.

Sometimes perspectives of other Sacramento city officials and agency leaders were overlooked in board deliberations too. The school district seemingly acted in isolation rather than collaboration. Several parent coalitions from organized neighborhoods; for instance, pleaded with the board and district staff to examine traffic patterns and environmental pollution before approving new school locations. On another occasion, parents protested co-location of a high school on a college campus.

Many were not surprised by the outcome, especially considering the strife surrounding the closure of Sacramento High School. As a result, the district initiated efforts to involve parents and others in task force efforts, committees, and public forums. Temporary changes were made and constituents reminded the board and superintendent to re-engage the public on a consistent basis.

Second, effective community engagement can be sustained and improved with thorough consideration of recommendations. In other words, all angles of an issue must be examined. Noted author F. Scott Fitzgerald once said that "the test of first-rate intelligence is the ability to hold two opposing ideas in the mind at the same time and still retain the ability to function." In general, I did not find this to be the case with regard to effective community engagement in the school district. In 2005, district staff assembled community-based committees to examine proposals to close traditional neighborhood elementary schools in favor of charter schools as a cost-saving strategy. My concerns were about decisions to close schools without weighing public opinion. This happened in 2003 when school district staff recommended the closing and conversion of Thurgood Marshall Elementary School into a military academy without community input. My questions were often four-fold: the rationale, benefits, impact, and alternative. How would students and parents be affected if their neighborhood school within walking distance closed? How would the local traffic patterns be affected? What would be the impact with shifting higher and lower student attendance patterns at various school sites?

Third, accountability is essential for meaningful community engagement. In this case, accountability means reporting about how suggestions will be received, accepted, or included in decision-making. At some forums, input might be received as verbal comments or submitted in writing. Governing authorities and community-based report cards are a benchmark to measure accountability, a measure of how goals were achieved. In March 2006, I wrote a *Sacramento Bee* opinion column citing reasons why I disagreed with the vote to close Marian Anderson Elementary School such as lack of consideration for advisory committee recommendations, shortsighted due diligence required for any public entity, and school-based rather than systemic decision-making. I was the only board member to object to the district staff rationale about a cost-savings strategy. With few advocates and no organized parent association, last-minute information sent to the local city council members, and a pending proposal to reopen the site as a small charter school, I saw the handwriting on the wall. Clearly, the momentum of the small school and charter school movement was at play and there was no accountability for community input. By penning the article and voicing my concerns at board meetings, I aimed to remind board colleagues and district staff to remain accountable for listening to the public and looking at long-term and broad-based implications for decisions.

 Stay aware of the big picture—including opinions, implications, and future possibilities—when you advocate for others. If you forget, the decisions might be costly or detrimental.

Strategic Alliances

The Sacramento High School closure issue, the high school reform movement, and the closing of neighborhood elementary schools had a significant final outcome. The "popcorn" approach to policymaking and gathering sporadic suggestions from constituents finally came to a head in 2006.

Parents, public education coalitions, labor leaders, and neighborhood associations, outraged over lack of district accountability and the board's general neglect of public input, banded together. They proposed and passed Measures J and K, two Sacramento region initiatives up for a vote during the November 2006 general election that established "trustee" areas requiring Sacramento school board trustees to reside in a given trustee area. In other words, there would no longer be elections on an at-large basis. This landmark decision fundamentally changed the landscape of school board elections making it more democratic and having individuals represent the community in which they live and schools were located.

This was an unprecedented victory, despite attempts to previously pass similar local citywide resolutions. Measures J and K required greater board member accountability, including seven different neighborhoods with one representative. Up to this time, the board included four or more members who resided in the same economically established neighborhoods. When I enthusiastically endorsed both ballot measures, my goal was to reinforce the need for equal voice represented on the board. The first district-by-district elections were held in the November 2008 general local election.

What can be said about lacking community engagement? How did I help bring about significant in-roads? How did I achieve success within an organizational culture that did not embrace systemic perspectives? What will every leader need to do to remain proactive? I recommend you stay connected with your constituents or client and rally allies. You will emerge as the advocate for one or several issues. Likewise, champion for appropriate vetting and accountability measures for decisions made.

Lead the Community

As a leader, you must exert leadership—taking the initiative, advocating for specific concerns, and making yourself available to those you serve. Favorable outcomes include open communication, reinforcing trust among your base, and garnering support with existing and new relationships. In your role, it is expected that you regularly attend community events and social affairs. For me, this meant attending civic association meetings, business and labor community events, and formal affairs, often what I affectionately called chicken dinner banquets! To prepare, I color-coded events in the calendar of my PDA and made notes about business or formal attire and the groups and leaders I might expect to see in the audience.

Upon your arrival at events, check in with coordinators to let them know you are there to ensure that your presence is publicly acknowledged. Also, position yourself at key functions—sometimes several in one night—to connect with the right folks. Be on time, preferably early. Stay late, as you are able, to network with others including constituents, community leaders, and new acquaintances. On a weekly basis, I attended most neighborhood and citywide business and advocacy organization events as well as quarterly visits to more than a dozen of the eighty school sites. Finally, it's also important to juggle attendance at multiple events in one day. To convey your leadership, make yourself known and loosely follow the same general procedures by checking in with event coordinators and community leaders. Your attention to these details will demonstrate your leadership commitment within your community.

 You will be successful by depending on a variety of skills—innate and learned—to get the job done.

LEADERSHIP SECRETS

- Listen and glean concerns to ensure that you are a champion for specific issues.

- Align your decisions with your leadership objectives.

- Define how you will manage involvement with advisories and other discussion forums.

- Identify your expectations of community engagement and what outcomes should follow.

- Take the initiative to lead others by preparing for events and scoping out key contacts.

CHAPTER 14:

Each One Teach One

Help others learn from you lest history
is bound to be repeated forever.

Leaders simultaneously shape the present and mold the future. Innovative and progressive leaders know that they have pressing issues and commitments at hand, but they know that behind them is the next generation ready to lead. Those in leadership positions have an obligation to share with aspiring leaders the successes, challenges, and rewards about their experiences. An effective leader with insights gained through Leadership Building Blocks has viable mentors in his or her life and also makes mentoring a priority. Leaders help others by serving as role models and teachers. In turn, they receive support from a mentor or coach.

It was once said that a mentor is one who "has a brain to pick, an ear to listen, and a push in the right direction." Can you imagine how resourceful it would be if every leader imparted their wisdom to others? Even more interesting is an important consideration: How do current and aspiring leaders align their experience and aspirations? Let's take a closer look at how leaders serve as mentors and how they are also protégés.

No Man's Land
Believe it or not, some leaders attempt to chart unexplored territory of leadership without an advocate in sight. Any aspiring or forthcoming leader must take time to learn the essentials. The guide can be one person or several and can be in different career fields. My mentors have been from arenas besides politics and formal leadership, most notably my

grandmother. So, just how do leaders pass along their wisdom? It is about serving as a role model and teacher.

First, leaders must pass along experiences and insight to help others. It is not simply about sharing experiences but about developing protégés. Helping others gain greater understanding is not simply telling about your experiences but teaching and guiding lessons learned and mistakes made. Some pass along the tricks of the trade. Others might offer inspirational words or pitfalls to avoid. This shows the importance of serving as a trusted advisor.

Second, it is important to support more than one rising leader. Since everyone has different learning and communication styles, what you convey might be received differently. As a protégé, I learned the ropes about the life of a public servant and community advocate. During this leadership role, I had several different mentors to help cultivate growth and development in various areas of my life. Each of these mentors had protégés of their own in their respective line of work. My mentors included several seasoned political veterans, community activists, academic advisors, business and labor leaders, and spiritual guides. Each had meaningful insight to share and each was committed to helping the next generation. While I did not find all the answers in one person, different resources provided helpful tips.

Passing along your insight and wisdom to someone else is an obligation. Why? Even though there is no written mandate, insight shared with others is useful, rational, and considerate. Serving in various leadership capacities previously, I found it useful to benefit from the insight of a predecessor. Meeting notes and reflections helped me learn about organizational dynamics, strategic approach, and political sensitivities. Likewise, when I assumed my leadership role I gleaned valuable insight from seasoned political veterans who imparted general insight about specific strategies on various topics. From this, I learned that it was best to take what I had learned and help others learn.

To ensure that your experiences are lessons learned rather than mistakes forever repeated, share and help enlighten others. Record information about your daily duties, trials, and triumphs in a journal or calendar that you can later reflect upon. Then you can periodically review this to determine the value and the lesson learned from the situation. It could be overcoming a challenge, maneuvering through a potentially fatal faux pas, or triumphantly garnering unexpected support. Every leader experiences unparalleled insight in the day-to-day events alone that provide a learning opportunity. Let's review more specifically how leaders can inspire leadership behavior by serving as a role model or teacher.

Role Model

A role model may inspire a single person or the masses. This influence is evident in example-setting behavior, expected protocols, and socially-acceptable standards. Those inspired might be colleagues or the general public. What is taught through example and in a mentor-protégé format? It might be charismatic behavior, information sharing, or visionary thinking. Behavior is inspired through setting an example and modeling desired outcomes.

 As a role model, nurture others and offer helpful suggestions about training and what's required to get started.

What comes to mind is my stint working on Capitol Hill where I watched and learned the formal gratitude expressed between members of Congress yielding to one another. Before and during discussions they addressed the presiding chairperson as a way of acknowledging his or her leadership and likewise requesting to speak. These were essential protocols I learned and expectations I had for myself on the school board. At first, when I paused and thanked the board president this seemed formal and awkward judging by the overt reaction from a few school colleagues including smirks, eye-squinting, and audible sighs of exasperation. Eventually, they learned to accept my professional etiquette for public discourse. What I had learned from role models in the halls of Congress was training realized more than a decade later.

Teacher

As the daughter of a thirty-year schoolteacher, I think I've learned something about the patience and nurturing required in any leadership role. As a youth, I also watched and learned from my diligent piano teacher who poured her unwavering grace, style, and tenacity to make sure that I learned various classical musical passages. With these two examples of teachers in my life, I learned about the importance of dedication to the growth of others. As a leader, you have an opportunity to groom potential successors and aspiring leaders, staff, colleagues, and the community. As a school board trustee, this meant that I was dedicated to outlining policy issues with patience. I also reiterated a call for systemic governance and recommendations for improvement with focus. Finally, I articulated problems while offering a list of viable solutions. People heard my concerns but sometimes I had to approach the issues from a different perspective. Who was the intended audience? It was my board colleagues and the public in hopes that my insight as a "teaching leader" might be a useful learning opportunity.

In addition to serving as a teacher and role model, leaders need support from those who are further along in the leadership journey. How can leaders find support from peer or more seasoned leaders?

Coach

Every leader needs advocates along the way. These include trusted colleagues and advisors but none is more important than a coach. A coach is similar to a teacher but more like a mentor who motivates protégés, inspires confidence, and provides specific support. Sometimes there are unforeseen circumstances and often this type of teacher helps impart some unspoken wisdom. It creates a forum to exchange ideas and to simply explore creative ideas. Recommendations are made based on seasoned experience to examine multiple perspectives.

Your Confidante

Similar to a role model, a mentor is a dedicated advocate. With a mentor there is a unique relationship that helps a protégé glean a more complete perspective than if left alone to learn. And unlike a coach who will instruct you, a mentor will tell you why. This includes someone serving as your advocate to help enhance your understanding and perspectives, typically through a dedicated one-to-one relationship. Serving as a confidante is about entrusting someone else with helpful input for decisions you are making. Establish trust with someone else who has had similar experiences. This is a forum for establishing a circle of support. There is an unwavering commitment to be a resource for you on various issues.

In the political arena, it is sometimes presumed that politicians serve in this capacity to one another. Unfortunately, this is not necessarily what I found. In fact, most of my mentors were outside of the political arena. Furthermore, I learned to provide support for other aspiring leaders during my tenure by giving one-to-one insight about various policy issues, interpersonal relations, and my perspectives on managing crisis situations.

Win-Win for Everyone

How we empower others will lead to future success. This will serve as a pathway for others who pursue leadership positions. Through my role, I was able to promote teamwork between colleagues and constituents but likewise shared the value of mentoring, role modeling, and teaching. If each leader took time to help others to gain something from lessons learned, it would help empower others and encourage more effective leadership. Anyone focused on Leadership Building Blocks should know that there is an obligation to mentor others to maintain future decision-making.

LEADERSHIP SECRETS

- Commit yourself to passing along your insight to another or several others.

- Serve as a role model to inspire others to learn from your success.

- Groom successive leaders through teaching them important skills and insight.

- Champion for new leaders seeking to understand the "what" and "why" of leadership.

PART 6

FORTITUDE

Part Six outlines strategies for how to make decisions when dealing with the unexpected. Sometimes you will be faced with the unknown and uncomfortable. What do you do? How can you be an effective leader in the face of adversity? When you're a leader, you must react quickly. Sometimes you'll be under the public eye. You might have to go beyond your comfort zone. Chapter 15 highlights circumstances where leaders will find themselves—loopholes, potholes, and craters—and suggests ways to move beyond them. For instance: What are some patterns to watch? Chapter 16 provides a framework for how you might handle crisis situations. Chapter 17 helps you understand how to develop your communication skills on the center stage and sometimes under the glare of media scrutiny. How do you respond to demands from the press? How do you stay focused and develop a unique style all while it may be yet unfamiliar?

CHAPTER 15:
Loopholes, Potholes, and Craters

Effective leaders skillfully manage ambiguity.

Dealing with unexpected circumstances in any leadership role is inevitable. Some events you will have no control over. On other occasions, there will be situations that might have been provoked. Nonetheless your role will be to deal with the situation and readjust your strategy often on a moment's notice. You will have to deal with someone with whom you have a personality clash. You will have occasional invasiveness from your doting public. You might observe systemic challenges and unethical behavior that reeks of immorality. You will need to find determination within to rise above it all. How will you handle it? How will you respond when approached with an unexpected reaction?

In the political arena, it was essential for me to maneuver in these uncharted waters. Unfortunately, there is rarely signage announcing these occasions and, as far as I know, there is no written rulebook for how to manage these dynamics. In Chapter 9, we talked about getting up after being knocked down as the test of any true leader. In addition to that, Leadership Building Blocks requires that you are prepared and think beyond the scope of the known. Here are the three circumstances: loopholes that just exist, potholes you will have to maneuver around, and craters you must avoid. How you manage each will contribute to your overall success as a leader.

LOOPHOLES

In any leadership role, there will be the unexpected sometimes coupled with a lack of guidance. What will you do without a clearly-defined course of action? How will you anticipate action when the rules change without notice? This circumstance is defined as a loophole. Webster's Dictionary defines loopholes as "an ambiguity or omission through which the intent of a statute, contract, or obligation may be evaded." As a leader, you will learn that there are glitches, oversights, and sometimes no rules on any given issue, procedure, or cultural standard. Sometimes this includes an omission or oversight. Sometimes compliance is nearly impossible or lacking. This vague, unofficial guidance and undocumented rulebook exists; every governing body has its own rules and culture. Players: Abide accordingly.

 Analyze all angles of a situation, or course of action, and determine the best way to maneuver through these dynamics.

Serving on the school board, I learned there were endless loopholes. These included missing, outdated, or inaccurate policies, misguided decision-making, and non-existent board interaction protocols. More than that, there was a misunderstanding about the board-superintendent governance with the superintendent providing direction rather than taking orders from the board. Not only was I appalled at the inconsiderate interaction during board proceedings, but I was equally as shocked when the superintendent at that time directed board members to make decisions without policy on the books. I found this careless, unethical, and offensive given the responsibility to reasonably govern decisions affecting more than 46,000 students and more than 4,000 district employees. What was I to do?

First, I made it a point to focus on improving our board communication. Our public meetings were clearly out of control with no rules to respectfully discuss an issue. My microphone or statements were cut off and board members displayed disapproving body language when they disagreed. At my first annual board retreat, I observed the agenda was focused on a review of policy issues and decisions rather than a critical board self-evaluation and strategies to close the protocol loopholes. Given the magnitude of the opening and closing school issues our district was managing, I asked the superintendent to host more frequent board retreats for our team to find a better way to conduct school board business. Other board members agreed and in 2004 the board approved a final version of board protocols to guide board discussions.

Next, since the board required a more thorough process to establish, review, and approve board decisions with corresponding board policies, I implored board colleagues and the superintendent to act swiftly with improvements. After working with the superintendent and several supportive board colleagues, a board policy committee was proposed and a resolution adopted. Since I was adamant about creating a more effective process, I chaired the committee during the later stages of my tenure.

POTHOLES

A "pothole" results when a hole is formed from a grinding action of stones or gravel, sometimes moved by water such as in a riverbed. As we commonly know them, roadway potholes are deep pits or gouges in the roadway that preclude safe passage. It goes without saying that your role at the top will be marred by unforeseen potholes in your leadership path.

First, always take note when a benchmark changes so you can anticipate or create solutions. A standard public procedure, for instance, became complicated when our board perpetually did not respond during the end-of-meeting public comment period. What made it so disturbing is that the board was starting to deal with significant questions of impropriety and then no one answered. State law precluded our board from responding at that moment to any constituent inquiry that did not speak to a specific board agenda issue. This seemed odd since the parent, teacher, or citizen had taken time to sit through the meeting and to share their concerns only to have board members with deadpan faces and no response. Halfway through my tenure, requests to the superintendent and board president were heard by several of us on the board concerning the public comment response. We successfully achieved some authentic civic engagement when the board agreed to have the board president respond with a standard statement that the board could not respond at that time but that the superintendent had staff notating the concerns.

Also, clarify expectations about your role from day one. Most notable was my awareness that I was there to serve others and respond to the public—via mail, telephone, or public comment. I stayed busy responding to inquiries from one end of town to the other with my time management and filing system but I had an expectation that board colleagues and school district staff would have a system in place. I asked them to share with me any insight. However, when I took office I was not informed by board colleagues, school district staff, or the superintendent at that time about board protocols and process for responding to constituent inquiries. With at-large school district seats, there were no specific schools or neighborhoods allocated for the seven-member board responsible for attending school events and responding to constituent inquiries. Instead, we were expected to attend events according to personal preference or constituent requests. In other words, responding to constituent inquiries was done at our discretion. This process of haphazardly attending events and responding to constituent inquiries was clearly an oversight by school district—a pothole—at that time.

 Anticipate unknown roadway hazards and keep your eyes open because you do not know what is ahead.

Third, to avoid roadway gouges, be realistic about what you can address during your tenure. This is true for how well-versed you become on the issues and how you allocate time to address issues. For instance, a significant question you must ask yourself along the leadership journey is: Will I be focused on a single issue, or will I focus on multiple issues? Becoming conversant about multiple issues will allow you to rise to higher levels of leadership with a broader knowledge and base of supporters, if you so chose.

Another consideration is whether or not you have adequate staff support. If you do not have the administrative support, you risk failure.

You might also burn yourself out by spreading yourself too thin trying to respond to all issues without the appropriate infrastructure. As I mentioned previously, some constituents wanted me to be a panacea for long-standing school district challenges—dropouts and suspensions, equitable employment opportunities, and city-wide improvements among specific community-based organizations. There was not enough district staff available to assist with scheduling board members, managing constituent correspondence, and preparing post-meeting constituent follow up. In other words, the lack of systemic procedures to respond to the public and maintain board member presence was a glaring pothole. After a few months on the board, I refrained from doing too much without administrative support or the result might be my physical exhaustion from juggling a full-time job and part-time school board duties.

CRATERS

Craters are bowl-like holes in the ground that result from a shell or landmine. These are deep vacuums where you might fall. In any leadership role, you will learn about challenges and problems that existed before your arrival. These include systemic challenges, unspoken dynamics, and glaring oversights. On the Sacramento school board, there were several craters, including questionable integrity and legitimacy of school district endeavors.

How can you be aware of these? Ask as many questions as possible about the historical and organizational structure. This way you will be informed about all possible challenges you might experience.

As we discussed in Chapters 4 and 5, it is vital to have your support system and maintain balance. For me, some simple but noteworthy advice saved me from falling into craters while on the school board. My father pulled me aside during all the fanfare and accolades on the night I was sworn into office. He gently whispered his fatherly advice, "Never compromise your integrity." I have always treasured that father-daughter moment. Yet, at that time I knew that Dad could never protect me in murky waters of politics. Looking back, this was the best advice I ever received to maneuver unforeseeable craters.

One of the most challenging craters I experienced while serving on the school board was the very public inquiry about governing board decisions made prior to my arrival. In April 2000, the Sacramento city school board voted unanimously to establish the California Administrative Services Authority (CASA), a joint powers authority (JPA), to provide professional services to the school district. Services included administrative and accounting support. In the unprecedented decision, the board resolution provided an alternative retirement system for CASA staff members, some Sacramento school district staff, and other California school districts. In short, the Sacramento school district staff consulted with the JPA for services on charter school proposals. These actions along with other allegations were cited as conflicts of interest, impropriety, and evasion of California State and federal taxes in a June 2003 grand jury investigation.

Details of the enhanced retirement system became public in early 2003 just after I joined the school board. A June 2003 investigative report was released by a coalition of community and labor groups. The school district faced questions from media, such as the *Sacramento Bee*, and constituents about how CASA led to inequity for school district employees resulting in elaborate retirement packages for tenured district administrators and pension spiking for the superintendent and chief financial officer at that time. In other words, the superintendent would have received approximately $40,000 per year with the traditional retirement system. He received nearly $120,000 per year with the CASA system. Later, a grand jury investigation found that there was further impropriety and evasion of California State and federal taxes.

How did I deal with this tremendous crater? First, I resolved myself to deal head-on with the public inquiry and litigious nature of the decision. After getting over the initial shock about a prior board decision, I realized that my main concern was how the conclusions were made without proper vetting. I, too, was flabbergasted and disappointed with the conduct of this public board and resolved to be an efficient steward of the public trust by listening and asking the tough questions during board meetings on behalf of the public.

Also, when allegations of conflicts of interest and impropriety related to the CASA issues were raised in a public report drafted by community leaders and parent groups, I listened. I read as much as I could. I asked probing questions to gain a better understanding about how the issue had evolved prior to my arrival on the board. However, when I made inquiries of the superintendent at that time, I was advised that the issue was not of significant concern. Likewise, the board president at that time talked over any constituent who dared to raise the issue during public comment. It became more frustrating when some board colleagues tried to quiet public outcry rather than listen to the concerns and outrage regarding misuse of public funds. Regardless, the CASA issue was added to the board meeting agenda once the media covered the issue and the grand jury took up consideration.

Third, while I was angered about board colleagues unwilling to initially accept responsibility for malfeasance and negligence with public funds, I had to channel that into positive action. This glaring oversight eroded the public trust. Steps could be taken, however, to bring accountability through addressing specific issues rather than responding with an emotional response. This meant identifying the issues and concerns and possible solutions. It also meant that I spoke with conviction about the issues without being punitive towards board colleagues.

While challenges leaders face, such as craters, can leave irrevocable damage, it does not mean that perspective cannot be restored. The opportunity to demonstrate effective leadership is to rise above the adversity, manifesting viable solutions for amicable action and understanding. Without this perspective, leaders subject themselves to become thwarted by followers rather than providing them with solid leadership.

LEADERSHIP SECRETS

- Clearly identify the unexpected circumstance.

- Develop a strategy to manage ambiguity and oversights.

- Identify changes to benchmarks to find viable solutions or alternatives.

- Clarify your expectations about your leadership role.

- Stay informed about challenges or problems to distinguish your leadership.

CHAPTER 16:

Get Help Now!

Good leaders always step out from the
crowd and beyond the confusion.

Without warning, something happens while on your watch. It could be an unexpected altercation, allegations, or some appalling incident. It could be a natural disaster. It could be concerns about the organization's financial status. What should you do? How do you respond? Is there a standard response and how can you be best prepared to handle the situation?

There are no safe havens from the unknown. You will have to deal with surprises at some point. This being the case, your best bet is to abide by organizational protocol when you respond. As a leader, you will standardize a process to be proactive. You'll have to develop a personal set of guidelines for how to cope.

In this chapter, you will develop fearlessness and coping strategies important to the success of any leader and another fundamental part of the Leadership Building Blocks. Helpful resources and tips for how to fearlessly approach crisis circumstances will be presented. We will outline the definition of a crisis, how you might prepare, what you might communicate to others, and how to adequately plan for future events.

Do We Have a Problem?

What is a crisis? According to Webster's Dictionary, a crisis is "an unstable or crucial time or state of affairs in which a decisive change is impending; especially one with the distinct possibility of a highly undesirable outcome." In other words, it is any emergency that impacts safety, health, or good standing of people or resources. Similarly, Polish author Richard

Kapuscinski once said, "When is a crisis reached? When questions arise that cannot be answered." Sometimes crises emerge when there is media scrutiny or outcry from affected constituencies. Other times an emergency occurs without you even knowing. I know. It happened to me.

One sunny spring day in 2003, I attended an annual elementary school reading program. I was dismayed during the presentation by school alarms sounding in pulsing rings rather than a steady alert that would have indicated the end of a class session. Teachers and parents looked around curiously, too. There was no announcement on the loud speaker about an emergency drill. A frantic staff member ran into the auditorium of one hundred students whispering to me and the school principal that apparently a gunman from a nearby altercation in the neighborhood was being pursued by police authorities. The staff member informed us that the school was locked down—shut down to foot and auto traffic by a metal gate—while police apparently searched the area.

Without bolts or janitorial staff available to lock the auditorium, teachers, parents, and administrators alike overcame any potential fear to focus on finding a safe area at the school site for the children while we awaited word via cell phone that the apparent threat had been resolved. Students appeared unaware of the situation and were only aware that there was a change in venue for the reading program. We could hear police on loud speakers outside and helicopters circling above. Fear did not paralyze me. Despite fears for my personal safety in this situation and others, I moved forward with confidence. More importantly, I was intrigued by the tenacity of the staff reacting quickly to ensure the safety of the children. Some had likely endured prior incidents in this neighborhood and school site which was susceptible to gang and area crime. We escorted the children to a secure area—a room in the auditorium with a bolted door where we shared stories and played interactive games.

After several hours, school safety officers informed us that the alleged perpetrator had been apprehended and the situation resolved. Seeing the children's smiling faces—happy to have a special reading day at school—was enough to remind me about the importance of resilience in the face of the unknown. The school staff seemed untouched and unscathed, demonstrating enormous courage and putting their mission to serve children ahead of themselves. They stayed focused on finding resolution during an unexpected situation, a crisis by all accounts.

The tenacity of staff, parents, and students during that crisis situation still stands out in my mind. It was one of my most pivotal examples of handling challenges with grace. While there were several other occasions I experienced as a school board trustee including physical threats and vandalism, all others paled in comparison to the courage I witnessed at the school that day. I had to remember that I was charged with a job to do regardless of adversity: to serve the 46,000 children of Sacramento.

READY, AIM, PREPARE!

As a leader, you should educate yourself about organizational procedures. First, this requires a commitment to prepare and develop coping strategies. This is a simultaneous process of considering a review of appropriate measures—emergency preparedness and prevention—coupled with learning to effectively managing your emotions. Good leaders maintain focus by finding a way to balance attention to issues of concern and remain calm, confident, and in control of themselves. This could mean taking into consideration principles about balance and time management discussed in chapters 4 and 11, respectively.

Second, as a leader you must gather information about what has occurred to guide next steps. I used the five W's as my guide—who, what, where, why, and when. Asking yourself and others these questions will ensure that you assess action and strategies that have been implemented previously. For instance: Is there a crisis management plan guiding efforts? Is there a point person or team providing supervision?

Third, you should correspond with colleagues, constituents, and advisors about any action planned. In my case, I reviewed, with the superintendent at that time, requirements for managing school site emergency situations. We discussed providing updates for leaders—school board trustees and district administrators—on the protocol for informing the public. More importantly, this included updates for parents about coping with school-site crisis. You may want to explore several considerations germane to your role and jurisdiction to guide your next steps.

 Effective leaders develop an uncanny ability to deal with unexpected and forthcoming situations head on by taking proactive steps.

Keep Your Head to the Sky!

Regardless of any emergency situation, you must be committed to stepping out from the crowd beyond the confusion. To be an effective leader during chaos, you will need to take on the role of guiding others. Coping with the unknown as a leader requires that you are fearless. Being a fearless, effective leader means staying focused and steadfast despite simultaneous distractions. This means you might experience a sense of fear—fear of being ostracized or judged or fear of not making the right decision.

As I became an effective leader, I learned to overcome the fear of not always making the right decision. Eventually, I learned that all I could do when responding to any crisis was to make the best possible decisions with the information I had at the time. I also had to face my fear of being judged, approved, and accepted. As roll call votes were taken and discussions were closed on a pressing issue, I had to learn to accept that some constituents were going to appreciate the position I took and others were going to despise it. Regardless, I had to stand firm holding to my convictions and get past the fear of others questioning my judgment call.

In addition, to be an effective leader, you must move forward without fear. You must learn to be fearless because others are looking to you for leadership, guidance, and support. Looking back now, I must admit there were times I was scared about the retribution my questions and contrarian comments at school board meetings might bring. There were times when fear permeated deep within during school board crises including the Sacramento High School closure decision, budget cuts, public outcry, response to grand jury investigations, lack of school district accountability, union negotiations to avert school district strikes, inequitable treatment for staff and students, and school district administrators' conflicts of interests. While I was not scared to deliver written out speeches and public comment offered on crucial issues, I thought of the voiceless students and parents, unsupported staff, and beckoning community members who counted on me. They could not speak up but voted me into office to be diligent regardless of my personal apprehensions. Likewise, your job as an effective leader is to look square at any challenge and be a formidable advocate for your cause or constituents despite personal misgivings. As a true leader, your job is to demonstrate courage despite how you might be terrified inside.

 Effective leadership means being fearless handling crisis circumstances where you must move back and forth between fears you feel on the inside and putting your best face forward on the outside.

BELIEVE IT OR NOT!

During any crisis situation, there will be different reactions. Despite the emotions others may show, your role as an effective leader will be to maintain focus. You cannot be swayed by circumstances. You might expect to witness and experience these range of emotions:

- Surprise
- Disbelief
- Fear
- Anxiety
- Panic
- Displaced anger
- Distrust
- Cynicism
- Blame
- Outrage
- Defensiveness
- Regret and Remorse

Encourage others to seek understanding during a time of
potential confusion and chaos. Exuding confidence and
a level head will help stabilize the situation.

The Sky is Falling!

A children's fable, "The Sky is Falling," is about a chicken, Henny Penny, who believes the sky is falling when struck on the head by a falling acorn. The moral of the story is to remain courageous despite claims of an imminent crisis.

To that end, how will you describe a challenging situation and alert others without causing hysteria? In the midst of an emergency, how will you communicate en masse to constituents or those you lead? Will you send out a press releases or some other mass communication? Are there others with whom you should communicate with about the crisis situation including peers, partners, or emergency support organizations? These questions should guide steps to communicate the unexpected.

More specifically, you should review or outline procedures for maneuvering emergency situations and expected roles for yourself and other leaders. Some questions to ponder: Are you expected to find resolution alone or with group input? Is there a timeframe within which you are required to address a circumstance? As a leader, there might be expectations, for instance, that you become the designated spokesperson. Others might expect that you implement a plan. Be sure to have a clear understanding about what might be expected of you the moment you accept your leadership role.

Effective leaders should ensure that policies have been vetted and reviewed with officials trained to handle emergencies. That way there are no misunderstandings about expectations implemented. For our school board, school district emergency preparedness policies provided the action required for board trustees, the superintendent, and senior district administrators. It also included recommended timeframes, emergency meeting procedures, and designated roles for communicating with parents and students and the general public. Also, in the school district, an electronic district-wide emergency correspondence system was activated to notify parents, administrators, and staff about school-related crises. An automated message was queued for distribution to home and cell phone contact information on the school district database.

 Commit yourself to stay focused despite the obstacles or potential fear. If you do, you will go miles in the long run on your path to leadership success.

Pause, Evaluate, and Examine

Once you move through any unexpected event, you will need to determine the effectiveness of the crisis policies or protocols. Taking a step back after the circumstance has been resolved is prudent so you can evaluate the effectiveness, set benchmarks, and consider future improvements. More importantly, this means setting a standard for determining whether or not these rules were successful.

Finally, it's important to review crisis policies on a regular basis. With a consistent timeframe to review documentation, requirements will always stay current. A reasonable schedule such as quarterly or annually reviews will help create a way to update your procedures and mandates. At that time, you might consider any revisions to improve how you or your organization might carry out safety, security, crisis prevention, and emergency preparedness, in general.

In the space below, write down specific advantages that might result from updating emergency policies. What will guide your leadership decisions and deliberations during a crisis or the unexpected?

_____

_____

_____

_____

_____

Important leadership advice while facing negativity: Do not panic. Any sign that an issue, vote, or news upsets you will make you appear vulnerable. It might call your integrity into question or cause greater concern among those watching you. I witnessed some school board colleagues become disheveled about constituent concerns of an alleged hidden agenda, backroom deals, and politics as usual. It showed. I managed to dismiss negative comments and took pride standing up for my convictions. The strategy is to be as sophisticated and savvy as a professional tennis player, for instance, who shows little emotion over a missed shot. He or she misses the shot and moves on preparing for the next play.

The following is a list of emergency preparation and prevention strategies.

EMERGENCY PREPARATION AND PREVENTATIVE STRATEGIES CHECKLIST

- ☐ List primary and emergency contact information for your organization's leaders (i.e., home and cell phone numbers, address, electronic mail, etc.).
- ☐ Review accurate safety, security, and emergency plans.
- ☐ Post and distribute emergency procedures and contingency plans, if you or other leaders are incapacitated.
- ☐ Develop and update regularly emergency awareness programs.
- ☐ Complete in-service or training classes about how to handle a crisis.
- ☐ Designate organizational spokesperson to discuss with media, constituents, and other interested stakeholders.
- ☐ Review organizational protocols to allow for emergency meetings.
- ☐ Compile a list of emergency service telephone contact information.

LEADERSHIP SECRETS

- To handle a crisis situation, identify organizational procedures by developing coping strategies and gathering information.

- Talk with others about next steps.

- Manage your fears by staying focused.

- Acknowledge the range of emotions trigger by an unexpected challenge and determine how you will respond.

- Step out from the crowd beyond the confusion. Move forward without fear.

- Stay informed about challenges or problems to distinguish your leadership.

- After the circumstance has been resolved, evaluate the effectiveness and set benchmarks for future improvements.

CHAPTER 17:

Lights, Camera, Action!

At the end of the day, some of the best leaders
say the right things at the right time.

Actors must be ready for action and unexpected paparazzi at a moment's notice. Likewise, leaders must be prepared to put their best face forward. As a leader, you will likely be under the media spotlight and out in front of others. Since that is the case, you will communicate through your stated or non-verbal message. What you do not say conveys a lot about your persona and intended objectives. At any given moment you can communicate more or less than you intend. Thus, maintaining focus on Leadership Building Blocks requires solid written and verbal communication skills beyond managing the press, effective communication styles, staying on message, stating the facts, and framing the issues. It's about how leaders learn what to say at the right time. It's about how to address an issue in a succinct but thorough manner. The following are a few essentials for any leader on center stage.

GOT PRESS?

Since Sacramento is the state capitol and the eighth largest school district in California, there was weekly news coverage about the school district and votes taken. Reports were about challenges including declining enrollment, charter school reform, and facilities. Not a week went by without a constituent approaching me to ask if what they had read in the local newspaper or heard on the evening news was true. I soon developed a standard quip: "It must be true if it was reported in the media." How then do leaders manage the press and inquires that go along with that exposure?

Thoughtful leaders must take charge and manage the press. It's a commitment to almost daily interaction with print and television reporters and other media-savvy experts. With training, you can learn how to convey your message, despite possible misgivings. It took me almost my entire tenure to become comfortable with the media. What I feared most was negative press coverage from the local newspaper, being misquoted, and that my intended message might not be clearly stated. In fact, my remarks were taken out of context and other times my comments were not even included in a news story. Over time, I learned a few strategies to manage the press:

1. When you receive calls from reporters, acknowledge the inquiries and return reporter calls promptly because often he or she has an immediate deadline.

2. Gather the nature of the inquiry and deadline, and gather information from staff and resources. Since you cannot possibly know every issues on a moment's notice, learn who on staff and in the community can help provide answers and insight. Next, draft a formal statement and then call back with a formal, concise response.

3. If you are asked to make a statement by a television reporter, collect your thoughts before speaking. Ask any clarifying questions and proceed with your comment including phrases or anecdotes relevant to the topic.

Also, keep your message fresh with the media editorial boards and reporters. By establishing a rapport through editorial board meetings or occasional follow up telephone calls, you will keep them informed about events, stories, activities, and meetings of importance to you. Identify public events and ideas that might be a great story to tell. For instance, I kept a calendar of important annual events including college financial aid application deadlines, the Read Across America initiative, the landmark Brown v. Board of Education decision, and national library media awareness week. Annual college and parent engagement fairs were always opportunities to inform the public and the local media, and likewise promote my advocacy for college and workplace preparation and self-improvement strategies. To build awareness about an issue, I made it a point to attend an event, present a resolution, submit a letter to the editor, and send an email blast to constituents.

Finally, use your proverbial pulpit to get your message out. With strategically planned message drops through print, television, radio and electronic media you share more about your objectives. This could be through opinion letters, press releases, and special announcements. You raise awareness by pushing the envelope and occasionally tossing tables.

 Make yourself available to the local media if you are asked to provide comment. If you are not available or you are not interested in making a comment, keep in mind that your story might be told from their perspective.

Do You Hear What I Hear?

As a leader, you are always on center stage. That's why it's important to refine your communication delivery style. What you say is important; however, it is often what you do not say that becomes the news story or buzz around town. Sometimes this might include your body language, vocal inflections, or tone. Be sure to monitor your unspoken language since all will add or detract from any message you share. Your public statements about an exciting new arts program will likely be diminished if you are frowning, lacking adequate eye contact, or neglecting to have the appropriate vocal inflections. What you do not say will be interpreted through your portrayal in print, radio, and television. For example, do you seek information or demand answers? Do you use a short, curt tone, or do you elongate your words to soften your message? How you interact with others can make or break you as an effective leader.

Leadership Building Blocks requires focus. You should pause before responding and speak with the intent rather than a knee-jerk reaction with emotion splashed across your face. Some questions to help you evaluate your communication style and monitor your emotional reactions as a leader are as follows:

- How do you express your dissatisfaction?

- How do you express shock, frustration, and anger?

- How do you express remorse?

- How do you express concern about a single issue and offer a remedy?

- How do you object to an issue, but clearly state your concerns?

- How do you respectfully disagree with a colleague? The public?

- How do you say no to anyone who asks you to compromise your personal integrity?

- How do you say no to anyone in order to establish healthy personal boundaries?

Finally, you should improve your listening skills. These skills are essential and include receiving different opinions. In public service, it meant hearing the public share concerns and having self-discipline to respond without showing negative emotions. Many times I faced constituents who lost their temper and resorted to shouting and making threats. Others used offensive language. Sometimes when people are unfamiliar with how to effectively listen to the expression of negative feelings, they cannot hear concerns being expressed because of a belligerent, hostile, or aggressive tone.

It's also important to conduct meetings and stay focused on the issues and audience. On more than a few occasions, colleagues held side conversations and other times they ignored a speaker. To me, it was devastating to watch constituents share heartfelt concerns and having elected board members adversely reacting or not even paying attention. A reasonable strategy is to keep a poker face while receiving information from the public.

Savvy Sound Bites

As a leader, you must be ready to respond in every situation. First, be quick on your feet with a sound bite. Sound bites are short phrases that drive a point and bring clarity through summarizing the essence of a lengthier statement. Some that I frequently used included "stewards of the public trust" and "maintaining the teaching and learning environment." By developing a list of handy sound bites, you emphasize core issue in a concise manner. During my tenure as a Washington, D.C., legislative aide and as a former Toastmasters® area governor, I learned interactive and direct communication styles.

 Refine your skills through public speaking training or a Toastmasters International club to further develop communication style fundamentals.

As a leader, you must be both concise and thorough when called upon to provide reflections. To accomplish this, it is imperative that you organize your thoughts logically. Stay on task and re-prioritize specific issues of interest. Occasionally, I spoke off the cuff but more often than not I wrote out comments through two different systems to be succinct and on message. I often quickly scribbled out a four-column and four-row table with issue listed in one column, the problem or challenge in another, my recommendation or solution, and then action listed in a final column. This peel the onion approach helped me respond directly to policy proposals. In turn, I also developed three to five bullet points and comments to support the main idea. Often my public comments were provided in numeric format for that purpose. Above all, both of these strategies helped diminish chances of making regrettable remarks.

As a leader you must convey your message in different forums. Addressing an issue repeatedly reinforces a leader's message and likens the phrase "strike the iron while it's hot." Speak directly to an issue at a public meeting, community center, and in a local newspaper or neighborhood association newsletter. In the political arena, for instance, many politicians maximize websites and airtime on local television and radio station programs. You might also write a letter to the editor to register your opinion. Part of my success was elaborating upon my dissenting votes in an opinion column and community meetings.

Just Say No!

Leadership Building Blocks involves proactive consideration to carefully weigh the benefits and drawbacks of commenting on an issue. As a leader, you set the standard for how your audience deals with you. For instance, by not always responding to every call or issue, there is a gauge addressing inquiries. Specific issues you comment on should be related to your leadership objectives. For me, it meant that I spoke to issues about equity, and access, and accountability.

Next, tie your comments in with your core objectives. Adding too many other extraneous topics to an issue dilutes your message. Have you ever noticed a "media-monger" posturing for television and print media and who speaks to every issue? In fact, you raise your effectiveness as a leader by staying focused. This process forces you to be selective and say no to issues not reflective of your core message. Having a statement with facts, concerns, and proposed changes will help you debate the issue and not extraneous factors.

Another Leadership Building Blocks skill is to make sure to define yourself. Sometimes the media and others will attempt to define you. You can say no to the definition established about you by creating your own image. Sometimes national public figures are pigeon-holed by media as single-issue advocates.

 Be mindful about when you comment on an issue. Anytime you make a comment as a leader you may be asked to further explain your position.

Communication Policy and Protocols

To be an effective leader, you must be familiar with the communication and community relations policies. This will help you learn more about specific roles for leaders and support staff. We learned about working with different communities in Chapter 13. To further ensure definitive leadership, clarify the designated organizational spokesperson. Typically, this is the public information officer, chief executive officer, or board president. Knowing who the key contact is will ensure effective team leadership and open communication when press have inquiries or the organization take proactive steps to convey a message to the public.

Unfortunately, while reading the morning daily newspaper one day, I learned that four school board colleagues, now considered the board majority, published a letter to the editor in the *Sacramento Bee* blasting the public for opposition. In the letter, they also dismissed me and two dissenting school board trustees who disagreed with them. Was my tenure going to turn into a 1950s wild western movie with dueling sides taking to the streets at high noon? I was stunned. Wounded but not devastated, two board colleagues and I fired off an opinion letter in response. A few days later our letter ran on August 7, 2003, in the *Sacramento News and Review*. Our letter to the editor also subsequently appeared in the *Sacramento Bee* and *Sacramento Observer*. We vociferously defended our dissenting votes and cited clear, rationale objections to the closure of the high school. Our opinions were backed by several labor organizations and parent groups also opposed to the hasty school closure. Interestingly enough, the school closure decision was later found illegal by a judicial court order not associated with the grand jury investigation into school board conflicts of interests related to CASA.

 Get media training and support from your organizational public information officer, trade associations, advocacy groups, and public relations firms.

Speak to the Issues

Leadership is a game of strategy and power. To ensure success, stay focused on the issues. This is neither a chess game where you study your opponents or a mock game show. It's more like a tennis game where your service (return) is to force the ball where you want. You use your own style to stay on message. You will be faced with distractions but focus and ask tough questions. Probe into all aspects of an issue and serve as an advocate. Do this by communicating the benefits and drawbacks of policy issues.

First, share your priority goals with the audience you serve. A deliberate, thoughtful message rather than a sporadic sputtering of concerns is vital when communicating with your public. Be sure to make numerous presentations on any number of issues and be a representative at various events. This will help you to widely disseminate your message.

Delivering speeches, making public comments, and writing out comments on policy issues and constituent concerns will become your routine. In my role, I did this several times a week at formal board meetings but also at school sites and community events. I prepared written remarks almost every week on issues such as school violence and safety, effective governance, school library funding, and equity and access. Consider creative ways to repeat your message in public comment, rebuttals to colleagues and presentations. Here are some successful public speaking techniques:

- Always state your name and your title
- Customize your remarks to each event, audience, time of day, and issue
- Use humor appropriately
- Avoid negative statements but rather offer upbeat solutions
- Be concise and direct
- Use phrases that engage your audience, such as "Let us…"
- Ask questions to stimulate thinking about broader impact
- Use smooth transitions, pauses, and emphasis
- Convey emotion through your words for effectiveness (smile, frown, grief, enthusiasm)
- Use visuals and statistics as necessary
- Say "I don't know" when you don't know

You might also analyze the angles of an issue and the potential implications. What you gather might be helpful for you and others. When making comments, always convey a few facts about an issue and tie in how it links with your goals. It might be helpful to role-play with mentors and colleagues to perfect your standard response.

Do your homework gathering background information, cost-benefit analysis, and potential implications. Check facts and get the complete context of any issue.

FRAME THIS!

Another important quality for all leaders is to prepare adequately for discussions. More than likely, there will be intertwined issues for you to examine and untangle. You must first frame the merits, citing both the benefits and drawbacks to help you make your argument. Without framing the question, you cannot have the desired discussion because there might be a misunderstanding about the core issue. Making policy decisions, for instance, requires examination of the social, political, and financial implications and corresponding rationale.

Framing the issues involves more than just approval of policies based on the stated facts. It is also about creating questions about the process. It is about how a final decision will be determined. As a trustee, I initiated a request for a standing policy committee so that the board would have more effective policy discussions with evident accountability. To me, it was important to point out shortcomings such as the lack of timely policy review that contributed to the ineffective governance system.

Likewise, you will need to develop and clarify your ideas. Prepare your analysis with notes about the implications. This will include rationale where you are doing your homework. As a trustee, I found haphazard and reckless policymaking without stated financial or social factors cited. For these reasons, I felt that there needed to be focus on how to address an issue. More specifically, it seemed necessary to provide rationale because there must be accountability for allocation of public resources.

In addition to the analysis you will need to assess the impact of your decisions. To do so, consult mentors and colleagues to find out if there is any overlap on issues of mutual interest. In turn, you will need to propose solutions. If it is an issue on which you do not agree, then you will need to lay out your argument. Just opposing a policy without rationale will not be convincing for colleagues or constituents. Demonstrating your knowledge of an issue will be evident at the time of consideration and

will also serve as a reference for you in future discussions. More important is the quality of taking into account different perspectives.

Finally, frame your response with the facts. Be prepared to be direct
and candid with your answers to each issue. Briefly do so in a public forum
and put the "rumor-mongers" to rest by dismissing their statements and
tactics. Carefully defuse false accusations tactfully to ensure that you are
setting a precedent and a consistent track record for handling negative
circumstances. By taking the high road you will address the issues head
on and stay on track with the discussion.

Asking the Right Questions

One of the most relevant parts of your job is probing issues and asking
the right questions. It's not about demanding answers but asking the right
questions. Review facts and get more information to share beforehand.
For instance, asking an open-ended question about details from agenda
items will frame the discussion.

Furthermore, before asking questions, scan the scope of the discussion
and carefully ask about a specific issue that adds value to a conversation.
Sometimes people can over-inquire and then it appears that they are bela-
boring every issue. Also, present alternatives and help bridge gaps in opinion
to yield consensus and have other information to support your assertions.

LEADERSHIP SECRETS

- Establish a strategy to manage the media and keep your message out in front.

- Refine your communication style including speaking and listening skills.

- Develop solid sound bites and practice handling yourself in different environments.

- Stay informed about challenges or problems to distinguish your leadership.

- Be selective as you respond and when you decline participation or attendance.

- Seek training to ensure you become a skillful communicator.

- Speak about issues and frame concerns to shape discussions and decision-making.

PART 7

GO FOR INFINITE POSSIBILITIES

The final component of the Leadership Building Blocks includes imagining infinite possibilities when you consider current and alternate leadership options. In Chapter 18, we will review the process for determining subsequent leadership terms or alternatives. Will you pursue a subsequent term? How will you achieve the next level of success? How will you round the corners, should you decide to tackle a successive leadership role? If you do choose another path, what is the process? Chapter 19 discusses the steps you need to take once you relinquish your position. Chapter 20 highlights how you can leave a lasting legacy and steps you might take to achieve more effective leadership.

CHAPTER 18:

Just Do It Again

Leaders renew their position by considering all options, recommitting, changing course, or looking at alternatives.

Leaders must decide at some point whether to remain in their current leadership positions or seek a different opportunity. To renew involves running for the position again or getting re-appointed.

Making a decision whether or not to renew your interest in a top job can be difficult. It is not one made lightly. There might be external priorities such as family matters or personal well-being. Some are pushed or encouraged by constituents. For some, an internal timer goes off. Others get a sense from colleagues that the time is right to move on. How will you make this decision? What are some key considerations?

As the designated leader in an appointed or elected position, you are an incumbent. According to Webster's Dictionary, an incumbent is "anyone who currently holds an existing leadership role, whether it is an appointed or elected position." In that regard, you have at your disposal readily-available support. If you seek reelection or reappointment to your post, you will likely mount a campaign that engages your kitchen cabinet. This informal alliance of trusted advisors, mentors, and allies helps you begin the process, strategize, and move forward accordingly. Alternatively, if you are mounting a campaign, per se, for a different position, then you will have a different focus. Finally, you might seek an alternative career beyond the scope of a leadership position. I chose the latter. We'll discuss how you will step out of your leadership role in Chapter 19. With any of these transitions, any effective leader will carefully weigh this step of the *Leadership Building Blocks*. Let's take a closer look at each circumstance.

To Lead or Not To Lead

A first step is to ask yourself *why* you want to either reapply or vacate this position. Changing course means stepping away from a top community or organizational position sometimes back to being an average citizen. Since this will be a very personal decision, you must take a critical look at your goals, capabilities, and interests. What best suits you given your goals? What about any family, personal obligations, or health circumstances?

From my experience, it is often assumed that when you get into a leadership role, you will continue to ascend in levels of authority. It is presumed that once in a leadership position that you stay. In my case, I was expected to inquire, seek, and run for the next level of political office. Some people shared assumptions that I might one day run for city council and later possibly a state assembly seat. Some even joked about me becoming an elected dignitary walking the halls of Congress. Nonetheless, I saw myself then as a leader committed to education initiatives rather than policy issues in general.

When considering if you will go to the next level or recommit for a position, there are questions you must confirm for yourself. For instance, you will need to determine if you have a genuine interest to lead others rather than simply re-subscribing for the position. Rate your interest in a subsequent leadership role as follows:

1. Do you want to serve for another term in this position?
   - ☐ No   1 point
   - ☐ Maybe   5 points
   - ☐ Yes   10 points

2. Is there a different position that would help you accomplish your goals?
   - ☐ No   1 point
   - ☐ Maybe   5 points
   - ☐ Yes   10 points

3. Do you have the energy and/or desire to serve in this capacity?

    ☐ No   1 point
    ☐ Maybe   5 points
    ☐ Yes   10 points

4. Have your personal or family priorities changed since you assumed this role?

    ☐ No   1 point
    ☐ Maybe   5 points
    ☐ Yes   10 points

5. Do you have time available to mount an effective campaign to secure this position again?

    ☐ No   1 point
    ☐ Maybe   5 points
    ☐ Yes   10 points

6. Do you have required resources or energy to mount an effective campaign?

    ☐ No   1 point
    ☐ Maybe   5 points
    ☐ Yes   10 points

7. Do you enjoy serving this constituency?

    ☐ No   1 point
    ☐ Maybe   5 points
    ☐ Yes   10 points

8. Do you have current projects that will bring continued value to your post?

    ☐ No   1 point
    ☐ Maybe   5 points
    ☐ Yes   10 points

9. Do you believe you can be effective?
    - ☐ No   1 point
    - ☐ Maybe   5 points
    - ☐ Yes   10 points

If you scored 90 points, then go for it! You are clearly ready, willing, and able to re-up you membership. If you scored around 51-69, you might slow down. Do some soul searching. If you scored below 50, then you probably better give pause and do something different rather than leading others in that capacity. Evaluate whether or not you should pursue this role or some other position.

INCUMBENT FACTOR

An incumbent likely has accomplishments and possibly unfinished projects. That being said, supporters generally assume that incumbents seek that leadership position again. It comes as no surprise that some think it odd when an incumbent willingly steps down.

More specifically, there are inquiries and speculation: Was there some flagrant violation? Is there malfeasance or organizational in-fighting? Why give up power and other benefits that come from serving at the helm? Why deny an easy path to a succeeding term to accomplish even more? Only you will be able to answer these questions.

Advocates and mentors will likely champion for you to run again for a variety of reasons. Some will want to see you continue the work you started. A few will see your presence as advantageous whereas others will be indifferent. I can recall the subtle hints and perpetual questions about why I was not running again. Why would I decline to run again if I was a clear front-runner and an incumbent? Staunch allies were prepared to make significant political contributions. Others who had become converted believers to my cause—calls for accountability—pledged to garner resources on my behalf and mobilize my campaign. Supporters fervently backed my political agenda. In spite of all the support and backing, I could not heed the call to serve another term because I felt called to do a different type of long-term service.

When an incumbent wants to continue serving there are several steps to consider. The first is to ensure a viable pool of resources and supporters to provide support. For an elected candidate, this means examining the coffers in the incumbent's treasury along with potential for giving from key advocates and organizations. Similarly, any leaders will determine the appropriate resources necessary for an official registration as a candidate. For an appointment, this will require leaders to check on the appropriate contacts and processes—forms or applications—to complete. Next, a leader should secure a list of endorsements from those who previously provided support as well as any new proponents. This will include specific individuals, organizations, forums, media, subordinates, and peers. Finally, there needs to be a strategic plan to result in successful implementation. Other considerations are as follows:

- Reinforce your primary message and clearly demonstrated accomplishments.
- Define goals for your next term: why these are important, how you will achieve them, and why you're the person for the job.
- Secure endorsement from supporters. These will be essential to secure your base. Also, ask allies to support your re-election campaign.

Incumbents have name recognition that can be said to increase their chances to prevail. Perhaps most notable is a secure base of supporters, likely favorable status, an existing pulpit, and probably access to the community and the media. This includes a platform to showcase accomplishments. A campaign is yours to lose, right?

 Interject your personal style, objectives, and interests into your role as an incumbent. This will reinforce what you will bring to a subsequent leadership term.

Examining Personal Priorities

When leaving a position, it is important to state your personal reasons for leaving. Sometimes there's an interest in focusing on different issues or serving others in a greater capacity. It might be that there's an interest in serving in a different role. By the same token, personal family or health challenges might preclude a leader from seeking a position again. This will depend on the nature of your circumstance and how you and your family choose to cope. Sometimes leaders step away based on age or health factors or conditions affecting family members.

Similarly, a leader might leave his or her post because of exhaustion dealing with a barrage of issues. Already the life of a leader is a lonely journey, standing alone for beliefs, convictions, and perspectives. Regardless of the unwavering tenacity required to hold one's head high and shoulders squared, there is occasional disillusionment. With the perpetual political hurdles and bureaucratic roadblocks, I took a look at what my personal priorities were.

In my case, it was a formal public decision nine months prior to the 2006 general election that I sent a thank you letter to my supporters. In March of that year, I announced my intent to retire after one term. It was a very difficult decision made with significant consideration about numerous factors. I also carefully weighed my ability to maintain balance while providing ongoing support for my mother who was suffering from debilitating diabetes and other health factors. Finally, I really wanted to further develop and share my leadership and professional development insights with future leaders beyond the scope of a political career.

Consider the Organizational Life Cycle

Another reason that incumbents do not reapply is that the resulting professional growth and an organizational life cycle are no longer in sync. If a leader has outgrown the organization or governing body, for instance, the experience is no longer rewarding or productive. Organizations have a life cycle, or stages, that go from creation to development to maturing. To that end, an organization can be characterized as forming, such as developing, and "norming" which is the stabilization of organizational decision-making and growth patterns. On the contrary, "storming" might be an uneven process resulting from contentious inter-organizational dynamics and external pressure. This storming stage might preclude forming or norming from taking place.

Similarly, individuals transition between various stages of leadership development. These include new or young leaders who might be categorized, for example, by time in a position or breadth of experience. It is difficult to broadly define a new leader according to a specific timeframe—several days to a few months—since each person brings unique skills and background to a position. An intermediate leader might be someone well-versed in his or her capacity based on a step beyond the new leader. In that same vein, a seasoned leader might be characterized as such based on years or breadth of experience.

While there is no set timeframe for how organizations evolve, it was clear to me that Sacramento's school district was in forming and storming phases rather than norming. When I attempted to get the board to further examine board policy procedures and to standardize board agendas and decision-making with established rules, it was like pulling teeth! Some colleagues did not see the rationale for revising board policies or making board decisions with accurate board policies to guide decision making. Since the board was not moving beyond forming and storming phases, I felt my growth was stifled. It was clear to me: It was time to move on.

Priorities and skills will change during your leadership tenure. Working with any organization, you will have to ask yourself some key questions:

- In what stage is my organization?
- What stage of my leadership development am I in?
- Are the leadership development stages and my organization aligned or not?
- Am I willing to move forward with this organization in this role given the state of my leadership development and this organization?
- Do I possess reasonable required skills, favorable allies, and organizational dynamics to shape this organization?

Examine your personal goals and where you are in an organizational life cycle. Doing so will help you acknowledge when you have exhausted your effectiveness.

By January of 2006, I had exhausted my effectiveness in a school district where philosophical differences were evident. How would I improve board relations after significant board division steeped in the 2003 school closure issue? My effectiveness seemed to be diluted by my calls for greater accountability rather than piece-meal reform. While I had anticipated being an advocate for student achievement, instead I voted regularly on decisions for annual layoffs and rehiring of teachers, school closures, and budget cuts to programs detrimentally affecting teaching and learning environment. My objections to excessive consulting services and efforts to recommend creative cost-saving strategies were met with resistance on several occasions from some school district staff and board colleagues. Regardless, it is important to step back and review your personal goals along with the organizational life cycle.

TAKING A DIFFERENT PATH

Not only was my professional growth objective changing but my personal situation had changed since I joined the school board. First, my personal dynamics had changed since 2002 when family health challenges were just peaking but not serious. Tending to my mother's debilitating diabetes and other health conditions and keeping a full-time job meant I could no longer over-extend myself for my school board duties, even though I found serving most rewarding. Soon, what I also realized was that my personal development was squeezed between my two jobs and family. I had forgotten to genuinely take care of myself.

In my four-year term, our board examined and re-examined our stages of development at public board retreats to assess our annual policy goals. How many times did we need to revisit this before we were going to do something to make significant improvements? Much could be concluded about the lack of integrity and public accountability demonstrated by a public entity: repeated disregard for public input, disrespect for neighborhoods, mistreatment of line staff and teachers, poor judgment cutting student librarians, libraries, and other resources, and chiding of pleading parents who dared to question authority. My effectiveness had run its course because my questions more often than not fell on deaf ears.

On more than a few occasions, my opinion columns reminded colleagues and district staff about myopic recommendations and short-sighted rationale. Quite frankly, I was disgusted. And with the grand jury and conflict of interest issue it became even more apparent that political positioning and evasiveness by some school board colleagues became the accepted norm. There was no excuse! More than that, I was seeking to have an even greater impact than one-time votes that dissolved into the abyss. My goals dissolved because of lacking systemic structure to support thorough policymaking. This is not to disparage those who choose to renew membership inside the political leadership ring. Rather, it is a caution to not just jump into lifetime politics or any leadership role for the sake of doing it.

LEADERSHIP SECRETS

- Examine your personal goals about whether or not you want to seek a subsequent leadership role.

- Leverage incumbent status and find favorable opportunities if you decide to lead again.

- Identify your reasons for departing any leadership position.

- Examine where your personal goals intersect with the organizational life cycle.

CHAPTER 19:

Stepping Out

Every leader reaches a defining moment,
a point of self-examination.

Let's assume that you have decided, like me, not to consider serving in your role again. You may have considered against pursuing any succession leadership post. How should you convey yourself to make this transition from leader to an ordinary Joe or Jane? How should you convey your departing thoughts? Where will you find the answers and who can help you? All of these are likely questions you will ask yourself from the moment you decide. More importantly, how you leave will serve as a lasting memory that will say much about your professionalism and integrity. With the assumption that you will relinquish a high-profile leadership role, career politics, or an elected seat, there are some initial steps you will need to take to transition.

Every leader reaches a point of self-examination and the pivotal question: What's next? Some consider it before their tenure whereas others do so during their service. Regardless, this is a defining moment and an opportunity to clarify the same path or a different direction. Proactive leaders will have in mind a running thread between various capacities through Leadership Building Blocks. For some, it involves stepping out of a leadership role or stepping away. As a political leader, I stepped away, considering alternatives beyond the next level on the career politics ladder. I pondered paths to take after my leadership role. Let's take a closer look at how leaders determine the next step.

Taking Baby Steps

How will you keep yourself focused on getting to your next step and defining it each day? What steps will you take every day to accomplish your goal? You will want to look at your circle of contacts to discuss your future plans. Conduct informational interviews and find out from others who have served in various leadership roles about their suggestions for leadership and support for specific causes. Given your mutual interests, they will appreciate your planning and intentions.

Stepping to the Beat

Any leader will first want to do an assessment of goals, traits, and interests. Take a look at your goals and discover where you find your inner strength. For me, it's about writing, helping others, ensuring systemic accountability, and a commitment to leadership development. Some questions you might ask yourself include:

- Are there specific goals for which you would like to advocate in the future?

- Are there qualities you learned about yourself while serving that would be a possible next step?

- Are there aspects of your work that you have most enjoyed and would find fulfilling?

- Do you have courage to look inside yourself and think about options for your future?

- Do you have any interest to reinvent yourself? Do you know where to start?

Given all these considerations, it's important to build upon your core mission and the work you have accomplished. You will reinforce your cause by building upon your previous role. By doing this, you will add meaning to the work you do. It could be about service to your community. Maybe it is about serving on a board of directors. Or, it could be taking a different role in your neighborhood group. Whatever you consider, bring into your next role the tools you've gathered along the way. These will be invaluable.

Ponder what you liked and disliked most about your leadership roles. Make note of what worked and what did not, and go from there.

Tap Dance

Leaving any job involves giving advance notice. Departing from a leadership position resembles how you leave any job except this departure is with magnitude and greater mindfulness about appropriate timing. It is much like a tap dancer attentive to foot positioning, timing, and pressure to achieve unique results. For any leader, particularly any elected, appointed, or volunteer post, departing a position can be marred by complexity about the decision, when to move on, and handing over the reins. Provide written notice—anywhere from a few weeks to a few months—based on the audience size and impact. For any public position, at least six-month notification is essential. In my case, I provided a nine-month transition for myself and those I served to adjust to my forthcoming departure. This allowed me to prepare for the transition and likewise allowed colleagues, potential successors, and the community to adjust.

Regardless of the circumstance, it's important to consider the timing of your departure. Be mindful about serving until your term is up or carefully weigh the implications if you must depart early. Only you can make the call, but realize different circumstances result if you leave early. Since you have taken an oath to serve the public you will be setting an example for others to trust in your word and the position you hold. Also, if you serve on a public board like I did, there will likely need to be a special meeting to approve your resignation letter and likely a special election.

Dancing Partners

How will the work you have started continue? Are there colleagues, staff, or others among your constituency who can carry forward where your legacy began? To make sure, consider how you will pass along some of your duties to others. You will have a successor but you will want to ensure that some of your work and issues are sustained. Delegate assignments, pass along tasks, and identify those who will continue your work after you are gone. There were key board members and colleagues to whom I passed along assignments. I was also relieved to know that there were members of the public who willingly stepped up to handle issues I cared about—libraries, literacy, board policies, and parent engagement.

Next, maintain your presence in public and your role. Much like you did when you entered your leadership post and learned the ropes, you will likewise want to gather information about exiting the system. If possible, glean information from predecessors who have moved from active to retired leader status. They will likely have insight about winding down. You still have a vote and a say; however, your lame duck status means your perspective may now carry less weight. Rather than including yourself in the future analysis, for instance, offer suggestions for future action. In many ways, you are learning to accept for yourself and remind your constituency that you are phasing out. With the board policy committee, I offered helpful suggestions for next steps on how they might update policies and establish a timeline for implementation after my departure and the forthcoming election.

With this new perspective, you are phasing out and it's best to have a standard response to inquiries. More than likely, some of your roles are being shifted to colleagues. Some constituents will redirect calls and inquiries to others for your assistance. Providing a blanket statement helps your constituency understand that you are declining the opportunity to participate in your role and that you will refer the inquiry accordingly. This was one of my standard answers:

> *Thank you for the opportunity to serve you. As you know, I have made a decision not to run for re-election. I will continue to stay involved as an advocate on education issues. I'll refer your inquiry to our board president and superintendent to respond. Good luck and thank you again for your support during my tenure.*

Dancing on the Dais

Make your transition with ease and grace. There is no reason to cause a ruckus as you depart your post. Remember the phrase, "Don't burn bridges." It certainly holds true in this case. Maintain your contacts who will likely serve as future business references. Know that your departure will possibly be shocking and disturbing to some if this decision was unexpected. Accept the reality that some people may even be glad to see you go!

My voluntary resignation was perceived by some as a surprise and disappointing. It was not my intention to shock but rather to make a decision based solely on personal reasons. Sure, there were some days I felt just that compelled to leave politics with a grand exit. I preferred to leave as respectfully as I had arrived.

Furthermore, you can accomplish your graceful exit by staying current on the issues, regularly attending meetings, and maintaining profession- alism. Constituents and colleagues will call upon you so remain open to being a resource. As you transition, follow organizational rules and keep up your regular appearances at events and other venues. Remember to make good on your commitments. As I departed, I made it a point to say farewells to colleagues, co-workers, and others with a resounding com- mitment to serve through my term and to make suggested future action with various board committees.

Consider making yourself available, as needed, and provide your follow up contact information.

Exit Stage Left

So how do you exit with courage, integrity, and mindfulness? When you depart, you should provide verbal and written notice and probably consider making brief, but sensitive departing remarks. Understand that you do not have an obligation to say much more than that you are leaving. However, it is helpful to provide some explanation. You will be well-served to highlight the accomplishments rather than the low-points of your experience. With this occasion, cite special projects and fond memories about endeavors for which you have been passionate. Upon my departure, I mentioned the significance of the board policy commit- tee and work that should continue.

Comply with protocols for departure, notice to key people, and paperwork that must be filed. In addition, you will need to return any company or agency property in a timely manner. Finally, you will be well-served to get recommendation letters, if appropriate.

Part of leaving any leadership post might resemble a divorce. It could involve feelings of separation and anxiousness, possibly confusion. I know. As a divorcee, I experienced some of these feelings shortly after leaving the board. Expected duties will no longer be fulfilled, the decision-making process will not include your voice, and some conversations about issues of mutual interest will cease. Regardless of the stature of your position, you will be at a turning point in your elevated role. If you no longer serve in a leadership position, how your community deals with you will differ than if you were serving in a succeeding or more senior-level position.

As you start to make the transition, you will probably experience many challenges, one of which will be that you will no longer be on center stage. That means you will likely have a less hectic schedule. It might be challenging to deal with vacant parts of your day-to-day once filled from sunrise to sunset with meetings and activities. You might even feel a bit lost with sudden free time. You had become accustomed to handling constituent inquiries, scanning weekly reading materials, newspapers, and periodicals, and juggling a sun-up to sun-down schedule. It's important to have a self-care plan as you exit from your public role. This might include taking an extended vacation, spending time alone or with family, or taking up an old favorite hobby. Whatever you do, make sure it involves taking care of yourself and not the issues and people you have catered to during your service. Soon your life will exist without these partners, constituents, and colleagues as you once knew it.

LEADERSHIP SECRETS

- Be mindful about timing your departure and transition process.

- Develop a comprehensive strategy for managing your exit.

- Maintain your presence as you identify your next step.

- Honor commitments within your community and with obligations.

- Manage the range of emotions you feel as you depart your role.

CHAPTER 20:

Legacy

"The best way to predict your future is to create it."

—*Anonymous*

Family traditions are passed along from generation to generation. This is how we learn about those who came before us. Heritage or some endearing quality leaves a lasting memory, a legacy. It might be a message or wisdom that is told. It is also permanent evidence and often something tangible. With families, these include artwork, heirlooms, cultural traditions, or relevant skills.

The essence of legacy within Leadership Building Blocks is about what will be left behind once you are gone from that post. For any leader, leaving a legacy could be a significant accomplishment, improved services, or streamlined initiatives. It is how you will be remembered. Leaders can propel themselves favorably into history books both during and after their tenure. Just consider some lasting examples from the noteworthy leadership of freedom fighters whose legacy emerged from their actions, speeches, and recorded deliberations. Historical figures include African-American abolitionist Frederick Douglass, revolutionary first lady Eleanor Roosevelt, and Mexican-American labor activist César Chavez. Each carved out traits essential for any solid leader without explicitly making a statement.

But first, some questions emerge. How do you want your leadership tenure to be remembered? How will you determine this? What traits will you pass along to others?

For me, legacy meant passing down stories and memories through oral tradition and storytelling. I often sat among my grandparents and

elders having adult conversations where I learned about my four generations of preachers, teachers, and community leaders. By all accounts, my
ancestors exuded variations of faith, integrity, wisdom, and extraordinary
courage. These were family members who had survived, overcame, and
withstood adversity. As I left my leadership post as a board trustee, I came
to appreciate these family stories knowing that I had come from the same
stock. It was a greater awareness about my significance as a leader and the
legacy I had already passed along to others.

Pass It Along

History tells the story about how leaders support other rising leaders. If
you look towards the future, what leadership traits will you want others
to learn? What could you pass along? With Leadership Building Blocks,
you shape what and how future leaders will learn from you. This might
include accomplishments passed along. This could be insight or mistakes overcome.

For me, this was sharing with others what I learned as a public servant
including achievements and lessons learned. To be most effective, there
must be mindfulness about what was done before, what worked, and
what might be further improved. Even after my leadership tenure ended,
a commitment to mentor and support rising leaders became more important to me. As I transitioned from office, I helped other elected leaders
get acclimated with the public servant role. With students aspiring to
public service careers, I underscored the importance of developing specific qualities such as humility, integrity, and tenacity. I also shared with
them effective public service concepts and winning political campaign
strategies. While serving as a volunteer at the 2008 Democratic National
Convention, I was further inspired by discussions there about training
and leadership development for future political leaders.

From my family, I've also learned about the art of passing along
insight. I come from a family with a cultural tradition of weaving ideas
together in an enduring way—through quilting and sewing. With
amazement, I watched as my mother, grandmothers, and aunts created
home-spun craft work from scrap piles of fabric, clothing, or household

decorations. This artwork was made for everyday use as blankets and throws but also for gifts and special occasions like births and weddings. Quilts included multiple colors, textures, and designs blended together to create something unique. Regardless, the results were definitive and splendid, making sense out of seeming disarray or refuse.

Likewise, you will need to compile your collective experiences into some fashionable patterns or collage to make sense of these themes that emerge. Lessons are there within the piles of scraps that represent your triumphs, victories, and shortcomings. As you pause to consider how to assemble your piecework, consider what you would have other leaders learn about you and your leadership journey. Good leaders leave behind a legacy and impart to future generations achievements and challenges.

 Enduring qualities withstand time. Identify endearing qualities you deem necessary for any successful leadership post. Emulate these during your tenure to help provide a foundation for future leaders to follow.

Determine Your Legacy

Every leader must ask how he or she will be remembered once departed from a position of authority. I know I did. Leaders shape their own legacy when considering how they will be remembered for their contributions rather than others doing so.

For me, it began with a question about what contributions I wanted to be remembered for making. Effective policy governance and systemic accountability came to mind. It was not just the thought of having my name associated with specific initiatives, but how I would be remembered by conducting a deliberate inquiry process. This included how I advocated for all students. It was also part of fulfilling my oath of office and commitment to personal integrity, not just about casting votes or providing explanations for the public. My legacy became clear through my dedication to a reasonable policymaking process with appropriate checks and balances. Even after I moved on from service, I am remembered for school district improvements, integrity, and accountability.

Second, you must consider what helpful insights you will leave behind. It is reasonable to assume that you will share with future leaders what worked, what did not, and what you might do differently if given another chance. Like me, you will probably share your specific experiences and situational examples. For leaders to have a lasting legacy, they must consistently and tactfully speak their convictions.

Third, keep in mind that some legacies are intentional while others are by chance. The legacy to be left behind might not always be apparent and may take time to be revealed. Athlete Lance Armstrong probably never imagined that his lasting legacy would go beyond professional bicycle racing to become part of the cancer awareness movement.

Remember Who?

How will you be referenced in history books? Will you be remembered? As you ponder how to pass along meaningful insight to future leaders, you will need to cite what efforts were noteworthy. You need to enlighten others about how you were effective and why. This will include programs, initiatives, and endeavors you helped shape. It could even be relationships reinforced. Your legacy passed along to others will be clear in what you write and how you advocate for a cause. It will also be demonstrated by how you handle situations, document your accomplishments, and respond to triumphs and challenges.

In my capacity, I was particularly proud of helping to improve effective governance and accountability through leading policy discussions, board resolutions, and facilitating sustained community engagement. My consistent practice of asking thorough questions was also noteworthy in opinion columns, meeting minutes, and news stories. I created a lasting legacy as a meaningful education advocate, in line with my family tradition of reaching out to others. Questions to ask about how you will be remembered include:

- What are the core accomplishments that could be cited about your tenure?

- In what specific ways did you make a difference?

- What distinguishes you from all others previous people in this leadership role?

- What mistakes did you make and how did you overcome these challenges?

 Without passing along insight for tomorrow's leaders, future generations are doomed to make the same mistakes.

What's Your Legacy?

The million dollar question: What will be your legacy? If history were on fast forward fifty years into the future, what stories will be told about you? Will the proverbial record speak for itself or will others tell your story from their perspective and not yours? For me, I know that I left a legacy of effective leadership. I played by the rules and maintained my integrity. People would mention that I helped others along and advocated for greater civic engagement. Likewise, leaders must create their legacies by being proactive and be committed to leave a mark on history.

Beyond any role is the commitment to lead beyond the leadership post. It's about leading from the inside out, taking what you have inside of yourself and helping others. It is an inner resolve to reach inside and continue to take charge of an initiative, cause, purpose, individual, or group beyond formal governing. The bottom line: be about something more meaningful than yourself.

My legacy was characterized by an inquisitive style and earmarked by dynamic courage to maneuver the unknown. Despite challenges and trepidation, I took the situations presented and created an intentional legacy—accountability, sound governance, and civic engagement.

Passing along wisdom and insight is imperative now more than ever. How can a mission or vision live on if it's not passed along with care? How can a protégé learn if not mentored and guided? Effective leadership can only be sustained as we ourselves aim to do more to fulfill goals and visions.

LEADERSHIP SECRETS

- Ponder what you want to be your lasting memory regardless of your stature or position.

- Tell your story and highlight how other leaders will learn from your contributions.

- Identify noteworthy efforts that distinguish you from others, whether stated or implied.

- Help other leaders learn from your legacy, as noted in the section on mentoring in Chapter 14.

- Pass along insight, lessons learned, and achievements.

Epilogue

My successful leadership legacy was unintentionally created despite adversity during my service as a school board trustee. The words of Booker T. Washington come to mind when he once said that "success is to be measured not so much by the position that one has reached in life as by the obstacles which have been overcome while trying to succeed." Withstanding hardship and maintaining a commitment to helping others—not climbing a ladder to higher levels of leadership—meant that I discovered success. For me, leadership success could only be measured by making a difference using my talents to help others, effective governance, and personal accountability.

My tenure started as a commitment to do more than was required, to listen with greater sensitivity, and to serve with more compassion. All I knew going in was that I wanted to make a big difference and do the best that I could. I sure did that and some. The result was that my public service—challenges, triumphs, and life lessons—actually became my living testimony. I'm thankful for the foresight and encouragement to share my stories and pass them along within *Leadership Building Blocks*.

FROM BEGINNING TO END AND BACK AGAIN

Intentionally I stepped out of the political fast lane. In reality, I had nothing but faith to carry me. With no idea about when or how my big ideas on leadership might be a resource for others, I just knew there had to be a different way than climbing the political leadership ladder. The words of renowned photographer, poet, activist, and film director Gordon Parks come to mind: "The guy who takes a chance . . . who walks the line between the known and unknown . . . who is unafraid of failure, will succeed." Hence, I became a beginner again returning to life as an ordinary citizen, only this time with even more idealism and visionary ideas. Shortly after resigning from my post, I pondered about forums to reinforce leadership development. Instead, I found an alternative by vigorously pursuing my creative passion for writing. There I satisfied my appetite to unravel concepts, beliefs, and actions and found freedom to express ideas. Already an avid reader, I paused to take stock of what I had learned and started to write my own book about self-development and improved organizational process.

Some people assumed that serving as an at-large local leader was not challenging. Others balked that a single term in office was not enough to learn anything. Many assumed that there is nothing more expected than casting votes and showing up for public events. Clearly, this was not the case for me! This leadership role was more than an incidental part-time job. Sure, I started as a beginner in 2002. I dare say I earned a doctorate in leadership development, effective governance, and public accountability during my four-year term. More importantly, the experiences I lived became the backdrop for *Leadership Building Blocks*.

Writing this book would not have been possible without advocates and critics along the way. All had a significant impact and helped me become a better leader and, in turn, a teacher and coach. If I really pause to ponder those who mentored me—both informally and formally—I realize that they had a profound impact on my development. You will recall from the section on mentoring in Chapter 14 the emphasis I made about those who took me aside to offer gentle, helpful, and sometimes harsh words that reinforced sound leadership. Without their support, this book would not have been written, and I might not have emerged as a trendsetter either.

As I mentioned in Chapter 20, leadership extends beyond any given role itself. Leaders have an obligation to help others avoid the same mistakes and to learn along the way. In turn, I have maintained a commitment to help others. Throughout and after my public service role, I challenged other trustees and the community to create a greater commitment to mentor-protégé alliances.

Finding Closure

A fast track to the highest levels of political leadership and power is what many people expected and envisioned for me as a school board trustee. My exploration into politics and a high-profile leadership role, however, became more about self-inquiry and systemic analysis than about jockeying for positioning or re-election. Some people have told me that I stepped away from a promising political career at the height of my game. Others believe I might be a viable future political candidate. On the contrary, I've chosen the path to teach and serve through my writing.

Going into politics probably has not been ranked among the most revered career choices. In 2002 when I ran for public office, I had the guts to enter the political ring and the privilege to readily share my collective analytical expertise. Who could have predicted that in less than a decade there would be an unprecedented upsurge in public service career exploration and unparalleled daily public discussions about politics? What caused such a dramatic change and interest in civic issues and leadership? I believe it was two factors. The first was the information superhighway including the Internet and social networking tools such as Facebook, LinkedIn, and Twitter and the blogging phenomenon. The other was the array of 2008 American presidential political candidates. Hilary Clinton became the first serious female presidential candidate since Shirley Chisholm and Geraldine Ferraro. Sarah Palin became the first female vice presidential candidate from the Republican party. Senator Barack Obama emerged victorious to become the first African-American to become president of the United States.

While writing about my experiences, I looked back closely at my fascination with politics and public policy. Interestingly enough, the two concepts are often used interchangeably but have vastly different implications. I learned that distinction during my years studying at Georgetown and Howard universities and my collective public policy leadership positions. Throughout *Leadership Building Blocks*, I highlighted the importance of analytical processes beyond the backdrop of the school board or politics in general. This was done intentionally to refrain from delving into sparring about public policy issues and partisanship but rather to emphasize personal development, organizational dynamics, and interpersonal relations.

Writing this book was also my way of letting others know lessons I've learned. It was also about finding my voice and speaking up with my version about a tumultuous historical chapter about equity and integrity. It is nothing more, nothing less. There is no indictment or finger-pointing of an individual or system. What I have written about has been discussed in public and is meant to be supportive for those who might explore leadership roles.

Sometimes I'm misunderstood when I harp about effective leadership. For too long, I witnessed governance run amuck. It seemed to me that leadership was about more than just about anyone assuming the title of leaders. There had to be a better way than anyone assuming a leadership role without appropriate training. On the contrary, it was about personal integrity and representing the interests of others. In other words, how can leaders really hold themselves accountable? How can leaders better understand the importance of relationship-building, balance, and leaving a legacy? What good is it if our public and private sectors do not have trainings, regular checkups, and reality checks?

A Different Path

In 2006 when I left my post, I easily assumed different roles—giving advice and making presentations in the community for youth groups and support for executive training programs. Stepping away from a public service career and not running for re-election was the best decision for me to foster my interest to guide other leaders. Through this work, I cherish being an advocate and helping new leaders establish themselves and seasoned veterans to redefine a path to success. Along the way, I continue to explore the relevance of personal development, relationship-building, and tenacity crucial for leaders to be successful.

Moving beyond the political arena to pursue a commitment to visionary thinking and effective processes has been a rewarding part of recounting this journey and writing this guidebook. As a successful community leader, I learned, toiled, and overcame painful experiences to emerge with a vision of hope to share with others. In short, I believe that solid leadership constructs must be in place in government, business, community groups, and faith-based organizations for them to work well. It should be the mission of every leader and groups of leaders to develop the best possible skills. Rather than absorb myself in policy analysis and political jockeying, I'm even more committed to shedding light about the reality, the ups and downs, and the "how to" about being an effective leader. Both new and seasoned leaders need helpful insight; *Leadership Building Blocks* will help serve as that road map.

On the Horizon

Shortly after leaving office, I noticed themes that emerged. When I described my experiences while making presentations to community and corporate leaders, future public servants, and youth groups, I answered typical questions: How did I juggle it all? What inspired me to keep going when it got tough? How did I build a rapport? Do I have any advice about strategic planning? I assembled the collective triumphs and challenges from my public service puzzle pieces and fashioned them into this book.

While I left my political post, I have still remained actively involved in civic engagement through political candidate training and leadership development. I am committed to supporting others in their leadership journeys through how-to-guides, coaching, or consulting. As a matter of fact, I've already completed the framework for several subsequent books about how to run for political office and maneuvering leadership roles within faith- and community-based organizations.

As a high-profile leader who has assumed life of an ordinary person, my visionary thinking prevails as I align myself with like-minded leaders and advocates who believe in a better tomorrow. It is my hope that leaders will consider *Leadership Building Blocks* as just one of many trusted resources. I will continue to support training and education programs and forums for effective governance. My leadership legacy now, through my writing, allows me to help create opportunities for future leaders.

If, but for a moment, I can improve how leaders implement a vision, allocate resources, provide insight, and share perspectives, then I will have succeeded. What if we each left behind helpful insight to have a sustained and intergenerational impact? Can you imagine the potential impact? We can only hope that this endearing spirit will be shared from one leader to the next. Only then will I be content that we have each contributed to create our own blueprint for leadership success.

APPENDIX A:

Leadership Building Blocks Template

The template on the following page identifies the seven Leadership Building Blocks used for setting goals, handling inquiries, and managing activities and tasks. Each building block has objectives to revisit in three-month increments listed along with the corresponding chapter references. On the following page is an example from my leadership tenure. Use the corresponding blank format on page 177 to map out your activities and leadership building block objectives.

	Objective
VISION	Develop a Vision (Chapter 3)
BALANCE	Self-Care Strategies (Chapter 4)
	Build Social Supports (Chapter 5)
	Balance Priorities (Chapter 6)
COURAGE	Identify Risk-Taking Goals (Chapter 7)
	Implement Practice Routine (Chapter 8)
	Demonstrate Tenacity (Chapter 9)
DYNAMIC CREATIVITY	Maximize Efficiencies (Chapter 10)
	Set Organization Priorities (Chapter 10)
	Focus on Time Management (Chapter 11)
EVERYTHING GLOBAL	Stay Connected (Chapters 12)
	Build Networks (Chapter 13)
	Cultivate Mentors and Protégés (Chapter 14)
FORTITUDE	Manage the Unexpected (Chapter 15)
	Handle Crisis Situations (Chapter 16)
	Improve Communication Skills (Chapter 17)
INFINITE POSSIBILITIES	Determine Repeat Performance (Chapter 18)
	Identify Next Steps (Chapter 19)
	Create a Legacy (Chapter 20)

3 month	6 month	9 month
Set goals for reinforcing school district accountability	Identify measures for fiscal accountability and policy governance	Reinforce policy governance benchmarks and program funding
Schedule time for gardening, dance lessons, family/friend	Schedule vacations and personal time	Set work/personal boundaries through mini-vacations and managing correspondence
Set exercise routine, commit to practice leadership skills in the community or workplace	Outline self-affirmations to manage adverse situations	Create comprehensive leadership routine with self-affirmations and practice
Identify training, staff resources, scheduling, and filing system	Clarify work/personal priorities	Revise consistent and mobile office system
Schedule regular email, telephone follow up; make referral to others	Identify viable mentors and protégés	Schedule coffee meetings, lunch, dinner appointments (open-ended)
Identify protocols	Establish strategies for crisis situations, examine communication style, make changes	Improve leadership protocols
Identify legacy (lead beyond your post)	Clarify distinguishing leadership traits	Share your leadership experiences with interested protégés

Leadership Building Blocks™ Template—SAMPLE TABLE

	Objective
VISION	Develop a Vision (Chapter 3)
BALANCE	Self-Care Strategies (Chapter 4)
	Build Social Supports (Chapter 5)
	Balance Priorities (Chapter 6)
COURAGE	Identify Risk-Taking Goals (Chapter 7)
	Implement Practice Routine (Chapter 8)
	Demonstrate Tenacity (Chapter 9)
DYNAMIC CREATIVITY	Maximize Efficiencies (Chapter 10)
	Set Organization Priorities (Chapter 10)
	Focus on Time Management (Chapter 11)
EVERYTHING GLOBAL	Stay Connected (Chapters 12)
	Build Networks (Chapter 13)
	Cultivate Mentors and Protégés (Chapter 14)
FORTITUDE	Manage the Unexpected (Chapter 15)
	Handle Crisis Situations (Chapter 16)
	Improve Communication Skills (Chapter 17)
INFINITE POSSIBILITIES	Determine Repeat Performance (Chapter 18)
	Identify Next Steps (Chapter 19)
	Create a Legacy (Chapter 20)

3 month	6 month	9 month

APPENDIX B:
Recommended Resources

BOOKS

Brown, Les. *Live Your Dreams*. New York: Harper Books, 1994.

Buckingham, Marcus and Curt Coffman. *First, Break All the Rules*. New York: Simon and Schuster, 1999.

Burns, James MacGregor. *Leadership*. Chicago: Harper Perennial, 1982.

Canfield, Jack and Janet Switzer. *Success Principles: How to Get From Where You to Where You Want to Be*. New York: Collins Living, 2006.

Cole, Johnnetta. *Conversations: Straight Talk with America's Sister President*. New York: Anchor Books, 1993.

Ferris, Gerald, Sherry Davidson, and Pamela Perrewé. *Political Skill at Work*. Mountain View: Davis-Black Publishing, 2005.

Fullan, Michael. *Leading in a Culture of Change*. San Francisco: Jossey-Bass, 2001.

Fraser, George. *Click: Ten Truths for Building Extraordinary Relationships*. New York: McGraw Hill, 2007.

Gerber, Robin. *Leadership the Eleanor Roosevelt Way*. New York: Penguin, 2002.

Harvard Business Review on Leadership. Harvard Business School Press: Boston, 1990.

Higgins, Shaun and Pamela Gilberd. *Leadership Secrets of Elizabeth I*. Perseus Publishing: Cambridge, 2000.

Jackson Gandy, Debrena. *All the Joy You Can Stand: 101 Sacred Power Principles for Making Joy Real in Your Life*. New York: Three Rivers Press, 2000.

Jeffers, Susan. *Feel the Fear and Do It Anyway*. New York: Ballantine, 1987.

Kieves, Tama. *This Time I Dance: Creating the Work You Love/How One Harvard Lawyer Left It All to Have It All*. New York: Penguin Books, 2002.

King, Jr., Martin Luther. *Why We Can't Wait*. New York: Mentor, 1964.

Kotter, John. *Leading Change*. Boston: Harvard Business School Press, 1996.

Kouzes, James M. and Barry Z. Posner. *The Leadership Challenge*. San Francisco: Jossey-Bass, 1995.

Krause, Donald. *The Book of Five Rings for Executives*. London: Nicholas Brealey Publishing: 1998.

Kundtz, David. *Stopping: How to Be Still When You Have to Keep Going*. Boston: Conari Press, 1998.

Lencioni, Patrick, *Overcoming the Five Dysfunctions of a Team: A Field Guide for Leaders, Managers, and Facilitators*. San Francisco: Jossey-Bass, 2005.

Lipman-Blumen, Jean. *The Connective Edge: Leading in An Interdependent World*. San Francisco: Jossey-Bass, 1996.

Maxwell, John. *21 Irrefutable Laws of Leadership*. Nashville: Thomas Nelson, 1991.

Monroe, Lorraine. *The Monroe Doctrine*. New York: Public Affairs, 2003.

Sipe, James and Don Frick. *Seven Pillars of Servant Leadership: Practicing the Wisdom of Leading By Serving*. New Jersey: Paulist Press, 2009.

Smiley, Tavis. *Doing What's Right: How to Fight for What You Believe In*. New York: Anchor Books: 2000.

WORKSHOPS

Dawn McCoy leads workshops and gives talks all over the United States. She also conducts coaching and training programs. If you would like to receive more workshop information, contact:

Dawn McCoy
P.O. Box 5506, Midlothian, Virginia 23112
Phone: 877-210-4049
Fax: 877-218-2954
Email: admin@flourishleadership.com
www.flourishleadership.com

About the Author

In 2002, at the age of thirty-three, Dawn McCoy served as one of the youngest African-American elected officials to serve more than 161,000 constituents and 46,000 students on her first attempt running for public office.

While serving as a school board member to the Sacramento City Unified School District, she sparked renewed school district account-ability. She initiated and chaired the policy governance committee and led the charge to preserve literacy programs and school libraries. She was a highly effective change agent who initiated greater civic participation.

During her tenure, she was also appointed to several regional and statewide positions including the Sacramento delegate representative to the California School Board Association, California High School Reform Task Force, Sacramento Public Library Foundation Board, and the Center for Teaching and Research Excellence.

Dawn ran for the school board because she was frustrated with how schools were preparing students for college and the workforce. She felt that more could be done to protect resources allocated for students to preserve the teaching and learning environment. Her goal on the school board was simple: improve educational opportunities for Sacramento city schools. In turn, Dawn wanted to reinforce more systemic and meaning-ful leadership.

In a crowded field of nine candidates vying for three open at-large seats, Dawn prevailed and won. The other eight candidates were "home-grown"—known citywide for their years of community involvement. On the contrary, Dawn was a Sacramento transplant of less than ten years and leveraged prior state- and local-level political campaign involvement.

Endorsements were vital to her success. These endorsements and diverse support citywide included seasoned political and business leaders, media, labor unions, and community and faith-based organizations. Public acknowledgement for her candidacy helped her campaign along with financial contributions. While she came to the race with several big endorsements she had very little by way of a war chest to fund the campaign.

As the youngest African-American woman on the school board, Dawn's tenure was distinct in several ways. First, there was a difference in the average age of board colleagues, corresponding household income, and social circles. There was no less than twenty years difference between her and the youngest board colleague. In addition, Dawn held a full-time job as an education executive while serving on the school board whereas several other board colleagues ran their own businesses.

Prior to running for the school board, she led career and college fairs as well as parent engagement workshops in Sacramento. Throughout California and nationally she was known as a staunch advocate for financial literacy awareness and programs. In particular, she led and mobilized statewide financial aid awareness in several major California cities. Dawn promoted college awareness and helped students and parents complete financial aid forms. She pushed for local schools to help students meet annual financial aid deadlines.

Dawn's journey began during the 1990s when she served as a Capitol Hill legislative aide and was a graduate public policy student at Georgetown University. During those years, she volunteered for local political campaigns and served youth and the homeless while working for various community-based organizations. These early experiences laid the foundation for her perspectives and non-profit leadership positions later held at national education organizations. Since 1993, Dawn has published writings in several national dailies on leadership and professional development issues.

Dawn grew up the eldest child and learned that women had a voice too, rather than just a traditional place. Coming into adulthood just after the women's and Civil Rights movements, Dawn attributes her tenacity and ability to articulate her concerns to a long line of family members. Her parents and grandparents were church leaders and evangelists, including her great-grandmother who was a minister in the 1940s. Early influences also came from her active involvement in non-denominational

Christian and African-American Baptist churches and childhood caregivers from a local convent.

Dawn was raised in the San Francisco Bay Area and holds a master of public policy (MPP) degree from Georgetown University and a bachelor's of science degree in psychology from Howard University. Currently, she resides in central Virginia.

Ms. McCoy welcomes your inquiries, experiences, and reflections about *Leadership Building Blocks: An Insider's Guide to Success.*

Send inquiries to:

Dawn McCoy
P.O. Box 5506
Midlothian, Virginia 23112
dmccoy@flourishleadership.com
www.flourishleadership.com

About Flourish
Leadership Group, LLC

Flourish Leadership Group is dedicated to supporting new executives, those serving or seeking to serve in elective office and political appointments, public administrators, and others in similar leadership capacities. Our mission is to provide quality resources to improve how people lead effectively and how they cultivate a rapport with others in the process. We provide customized one-to-one coaching for individuals and consulting for non-profit organizations.

To request our latest newsletter and to be added to our mailing list, please contact:

Flourish Leadership Group, LLC
P.O. Box 5506
Midlothian, Virginia 23112
Telephone: 877-210-4049
Fax: 877-218-2954
www.flourishleadership.com

For more information about coaching, consulting, workshops, and leadership development, please contact us via email at admin@flourishleadership.com.

Endnotes/Bibliography

CHAPTER 1

Sacramento Bee, "Playing It Cautious: Some 911 Calls Stretch Definition of Emergency," September 17, 2003.

Time Magazine, Ron Stodghill and Amanda Bower. "Where Everyone's a Minority" September 2, 2002.

CHAPTER 4

Rayner, B.L., Life of Jefferson listed at http://etext.virginia.edu/jefferson/biog/

BrainyQuote.com

Kundtz, David. *Stopping: How to Be Still When You Have to Keep Going.* Boston: Conari Press, 1998.

CHAPTER 10

Sacramento Bee, "Sac High Closure Frees School from Teachers Pact" January 27, 2003.

CHAPTER 13

Maxwell, John. *21 Irrefutable Laws of Leadership.* Nashville: Thomas Nelson, 1991.

Sacramento Bee, March 2006

CHAPTER 17

Sacramento News and Review, August 7, 2003.

Quick Order Form

Order online at www.flourishpublishing.com

By e-mail: orders@flourishpublishing.com
By phone: 877-210-4049
By fax: 877-218-2954
By mail: Send this form to P.O. Box 5506, Midlothian, VA 23112

U.S. $14.95

☐ Send me ___copies of *Leadership Building Blocks: An Insider's Guide to Success*

☐ Send me FREE information on:

       ☐ Other Books   ☐ Mailing Lists

    ☐ Speaking/Seminars   ☐ Consulting   ☐ Coaching Services

Name: _____

Address: _____

City: _____ State: _____ Zip: _____

Telephone: _____

Email address: _____

Other leadership development topics of interest:

_____

_____

_____

Breinigsville, PA USA
16 April 2010
236240BV00002B/1/P